Mysteries of
Lost Empires

Mysteries of Lost Empires

Marshall Jon Fisher
and David E. Fisher

First published in 2000 by Channel 4 Books, an imprint of
Macmillan Publishers Ltd, 25 Eccleston Place, London,
SW1W 9NF and Basingstoke

Associated companies throughout the world

www.macmillan.co.uk

ISBN 0 7522 1606 6

This book is published to accompany the television series *Mysteries of Lost
Empires*, a NOVA production by WGBH in association with Channel 4
and La Cinquième.
Executive producer: Michael Barnes
Producers: Michael Barnes
          Liesl Clark
          Julia Cort
          Nancy Linde

9 8 7 6 5 4 3 2 1

A CIP catalogue record for this book is available from the British Library

Design by DW Design, London. www.dwdesign.co.uk
Printed by Bath Press

CONTENTS

INTRODUCTION

In 1947 Norwegian archaeologist Thor Heyerdahl captured headlines – and imaginations – around the world when he built a raft out of balsa logs and set sail with five fellow Norwegians on a 101-day journey for 4300 miles across the Pacific. His was the first venture into a field now known as experimental archaeology, in which scholars assess their ideas about the past by subjecting them to the ultimate test. Heyerdahl's goal was to show that the islands of the South Pacific – particularly Easter Island – could have been settled by people from South America. Most evidence now suggests that his theory was wrong. But the wonderful human drama of the voyage left a lasting imprint on the discipline of archaeology – and on the future career of a boy of nine.

As a small boy growing up in the Black Mountains of Wales, I was so inspired by pictures of Heyerdahl's raft, the *Kon-Tiki*, that I persuaded by father to help me build my own raft to sail across Llangorse Lake near my home. The raft proved very difficult to steer and in the end, like Heyerdahl, I just drifted. But building the raft gave me a great appreciation of the difficulties of translating theory into practice – my first lesson in experimental archaeology.

Decades later, as a television producer, I am still fascinated by the adventure of re-creating the past and the human drama of capturing science in action. My own ventures putting experimental archaeology on film began in 1992, when producers of the PBS series NOVA asked me to produce a programme on the Great Pyramids of Egypt. The assignment worried me. There were so many different theories on how the pyramids might have been built, put forward by all kinds of people: historians, archaeologists, architects, engineers, stonemasons and sculptors. How could we convey these complicated issues to a television audience? And how to make a visually interesting and dynamic film about objects as enormous, impassive and inanimate as the pyramids?

Remembering the response generated by Heyerdahl's voyages, the answer became clear: to assemble a team of experts, challenge them to build their own pyramid using only ancient tools and techniques, and film the result. The

television programme that documented this experiment, *This Old Pyramid*, won a tremendous reception on both sides of the Atlantic and encouraged NOVA to commission me to produce four more documentaries on the engineering genius of the ancients. These four documentaries, together with a rebroadcast of *This Old Pyramid*, became the first *Lost Empires* television series, which aired in Britain in 1996 and in the United States in 1997.

The first of these documentaries, 'Stonehenge', explored how the Stone Age people of Britain dragged enormous stones over 20 miles of rolling hills and erected them according to a precise solar alignment. 'Inca' investigated how those ancient people, lacking any knowledge of the arch, the wheel, mathematics or writing, built magnificent temples and fortresses from huge, interlocking blocks of stone and wove gossamer grass bridges to span deep chasms. 'Colosseum' drew on the talents of circus tent riggers, among others, to show how the Romans raised the biggest 'big top' of all: the amazing awning that shielded the arena during gladiatorial combat. And 'Obelisk' struggled to explain how the ancient Egyptians used rope, dirt, sticks and stone to carve and raise solid granite monoliths weighing hundreds of tons. This last experiment proved the most challenging of all, and our method for raising a 40-ton replica of an obelisk ended in failure. But as the NOVA team waited in the airport at Aswan for the plane to take us home, all we could talk about was one thing: how next time we would get it right.

And so the second *Lost Empires* series was born. In planning five new programmes, a return to the problem of obelisk-raising was an obvious choice. The pharaohs of the New Kingdom raised these spires in honour of the sun god, Amun-Ra. Only six ancient obelisks taller than 30 feet remain standing in Egypt and of these, only three are still standing on the site where they were originally erected. Clues to the process can be gleaned from a faded tomb painting and a single written reference in a papyrus scroll. NOVA asked engineer Mark Whitby, hero of our earlier Stonehenge experiment, to draft a new method for raising a large obelisk. He chose to use a massive wooden frame rigged with rope to give pullers more leverage. This would be the first experiment in our next series.

Opposite The obelisk of Rameses II stands at the entrance of the temple at Luxor. Only a few clues remain to suggest how the Egyptians transported and erected these slender spires of solid stone.

This medieval depiction of a trebuchet from the thirteenth-century Cantigas de Santa Maria makes it hard to determine accurately the size and proportions of the legendary machine. Was it really as powerful and accurate as written accounts suggest?

To choose the remaining four stories, my co-producers and I sought examples of other vanished technologies that would stir the imagination and compel the attention of television viewers. We turned first to the mystery that inspired Thor Heyerdahl: the unique civilization that once flourished in splendid isolation on Easter Island. Famous for its *moai* – the enormous, elongated heads carved of volcanic rock that tower over its landscape – the tiny, barren island that its inhabitants call Rapa Nui has long captured the imaginations of outsiders. The *moai* are arranged in rows on *ahu*, or platforms, along the coast, gazing inland with rather bleak, unhappy expressions, as if they smelt something bad. Others rest half-carved in the quarry where they were dug or lie abandoned on the way to the shore. Numerous archaeologists have attempted to demonstrate how the ancient Rapanuians might have transported the *moai* from the quarry to the shore and raised them upright. But none has succeeded in finding a transportation method that is historically accurate, viable and efficient. An archaeologist and Easter Island expert named Jo Anne Van Tilburg floated a suggestion: to apply ancient Polynesian canoeing technology to the problem of land transport. The NOVA team enlisted her help and tested this approach in our second experiment.

Fourteenth-century Scotland provided the setting for NOVA's next story. In 1304, Edward I of England sought forcibly to unite his own kingdom with that of Scotland. To do so he had to lay siege to a series of well-defended Scottish castles. At the gateway to the highlands, atop a rocky crag, lay Stirling Castle, the remains of which can still be seen today. But the weapon that gave its Scottish defenders the *coup de grâce* has vanished into history – all that remains is the legend of a siege machine called Warwolf. Historians believe Warwolf was a trebuchet, a huge missile-hurling machine vaguely akin to a catapult. But they know very little about how this kind of machine actually worked. In the matter of trebuchets, it is difficult to separate fact from fiction. Written descriptions of their formidable power and accuracy defy credibility; medieval manuscripts offer distorted and unreliable visual images. Nonetheless, NOVA found several experts willing to attempt the reconstruction of two types of trebuchet on the site of Castle Urquhart, overlooking Loch Ness. Renaud Beffeyte, a French carpenter skilled in *compagnonnage* (the art of historical reconstruction), believed he could build a trebuchet powered by a swinging counterweight, based on fragments of a medieval design by Villard de Honnecourt, a thirteenth-century engineer. Hew Kennedy, a Shropshire farmer, and Colonel Wayne Neel, a professor of mechanical engineering at the Virginia Military Institute, teamed up to build a fixed-weight trebuchet based on an illumination from a Spanish manuscript, *Cantigas de Santa Maria*. As part of the experiment, NOVA built a short section of an authentic, 5-foot-thick castle wall to serve as a target, so the two teams could put legend to the test. At a range of 200 yards, the small size of the target made the task of hitting the wall akin to achieving a hole in one in golf.

Like the trebuchet, the rainbow bridge of the Song dynasty in China survives only on paper, in this case as a detail of a beautifully painted scroll that portrays the city of Kaifung. Its design, totally unfamiliar to western engineers, is difficult to categorize: elegant, strong and economical, it intertwines short pieces of wood to bridge a considerable span. The timbers appear to be held together by the forces of compression, and the joints are secured by bamboo straps. All of the hundred or so rainbow bridges that existed a millennium ago during the Song dynasty have long since been replaced by bridges made of stone. But twenty years ago, Chinese engineer Tang Huan Cheng discovered a bridge in an isolated region of Zhejiang province that he recognized as a type of rainbow bridge. The NOVA team proposed that he use this bridge as a guide to build a Song-style rainbow bridge over a busy canal in the town of Jinze on the outskirts of Shanghai. One twist: as Song dynasty authorities probably required, the bridge must be built in such a way as not to disrupt boat traffic on the canal. This became the fourth show of the series.

More familiar to Western observers are the engineering accomplishments of the Roman empire. The laboratory in which Roman engineers perfected the use of innovative principles, materials and technologies was the Roman bath. The centre of Roman social life, baths were built by the thousand across the empire. Even the simplest baths offered several rooms and bathing pools heated to different temperatures. Much of what we know about their complex systems of heating and plumbing comes from the excavation of ruined baths. But one key element is often missing: the roof. Without a clear explanation of how the Romans vented their baths – how the gases that heated the walls and floor were drawn upward and kept in circulation – there is no way to understand how a Roman bath really worked. Fikret Yegül, an archaeologist who is perhaps the world's leading expert on baths, agreed to work with NOVA's team of experts to build an authentic Roman bath near the site of the ancient city of Sardis in Turkey – and promised that they could sample its pleasures together.

The rules for each of these experiments were the same: participants could use modern technology to design and test their proposed solutions, but only authentic tools, techniques and materials to implement them. For instance, Max Fordham, an engineer who is one of the world's foremost experts on heating and ventilation, used a technique called computational fluid dynamics to try to predict how well Yegül's design for a Roman bath would work. But in building the bath, the team was constrained to use only materials the Romans would have used – a constraint that caused a series of problems when it came to manufacturing the authentic Roman-style tiles that were to support the floor.

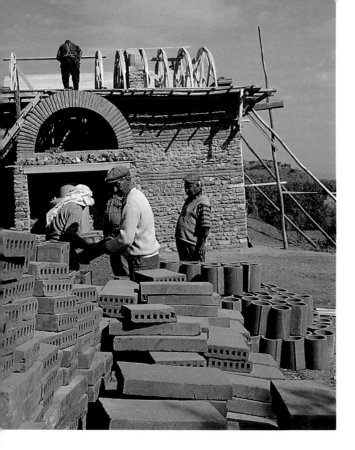

The Roman bath was a laboratory for innovation in construction and engineering. In building the NOVA bath, engineers and archaeologists strove for authenticity in everything from its vaulted roofs to its complex heating and ventilation systems.

To ensure a balance between practical experience and academic expertise, NOVA assembled a team of experts from a cross-section of disciplines for each experiment. This cross-fertilization is essential to unravelling the technological mysteries of vanished civilizations. Though they may not have had advanced science to guide them, many of these societies had two great resources: labour and time. This allowed them to use trial and error to find the most efficient solutions to complex engineering problems. Conversely, applying advanced science from a variety of disciplines can help archaeologists and historians try to deduce what those solutions must have been. Thus robotics expert Zvi Shiller's use of computer-aided design can help archaeologists like Jo Anne Van Tilburg determine which paths the ancient Rapanuians were most likely to have followed in moving their *moai*, and engineer Wayne Neel can help historians determine whether the fixed trebuchet was likely to have been equipped with wheels.

Similarly, practical experience offers a valuable counterweight to abstract theory. Stonemason Roger Hopkins was not shy about calling attention to the limitations of the complex engineering solutions proposed by Mark Whitby on the obelisk project. And engineer Teoman Yalçinkaya worked closely with archaeologist Yegül to ensure that his specifications for the Roman bath remained within the bounds of feasibility.

This mixture of perspectives can be a combustible one. When we started the series, we never imagined how upset and excited people could get about something as inanimate as stone or as seemingly abstract as the temperature of a Roman bath. Experts in one discipline often don't like to hear their ideas challenged by experts in another. Add in the stress of working with tight deadlines, unpredictable conditions and one's professional pride on the line, and tempers fray quickly. This can make for good television, but difficult working conditions for people who are living at close quarters for two or three weeks at a stretch. Sometimes this kind of conflict can be instructive: on Easter Island, for example, clashes of personality and perspective brought new insight into the kinds of tensions that may ultimately have led to the collapse of the civilization that built the *moai*.

The stresses of the project were felt by the filmmakers as well. Safety was our most serious concern, especially when dealing with massive objects and propulsive weapons. The fact that we often had large numbers of people communicating across language barriers didn't make matters easier. And there were more mundane pressures. With the clock ticking and bills mounting, there was endless cause for worry. All of the projects fell behind schedule at one point or another. Weather was often the cause of the delay. In Egypt, the *khamasin*, or fifty-day wind, blew in just as we prepared to begin raising the obelisk. (Fortunately it didn't last as long as advertised.) The trebuchet team had to contend with icy rain and frozen mud that caused hands to numb, rope to fray, wheels to slip. Days of rain also delayed the drying of the thick layers of mortar and concrete that coated our Roman bath.

Given the constraints of time, budget, and safety – many of which may have been of less concern to the ancients than to us – it's not surprising that on occasion we turned to less-than-ancient solutions. A crane here, a little silicon sealant there… the decision to make these kinds of shortcuts was always controversial. But cavils and quibbles were soon forgotten as each team faced its moment of truth: would the trebuchet fire when the trigger mechanism was released, and would the ball hit its target? Would the bath's roof stay up as the planking was pulled down? Would the furnace light and the building heat without cracking? Sometimes the ultimate moment was anticlimactic, as when the erect *moai*, proudly crowned with its one-ton *pukao*, settled into place with a gentle sigh. And sometimes the defining moment was one of defeat – and a renewed determination to try again.

One of the most delightful aspects of filming the series was the feeling of being transported in time. As I walked through the work site at Castle Urquhart, the ringing of chisels against granite, the smell of woodsmoke and the squelch of

These ancient statues, whose brooding faces gaze inland along the shore of Easter Island, have mystified historians and archaeologists for centuries. Many have experimented with different methods of moving and raising the moai, but the NOVA team was first to apply Pacific islanders' seafaring technology to the problem.

mud beneath my feet could almost persuade me that I was walking through the camp of a fourteenth-century siege army – an image contradicted only by the blue jeans and colourful flannel shirts worn by the timber framers who had joined the experiment. (Though perhaps the timber framers' accommodation in a converted monastery – with its lack of adequate heat and plumbing – helped them stay in character.)

When one considers the effort that goes into conducting these experiments (not to mention making documentaries about them), one cannot but admire the organizational skills of the ancient engineers. To round up prodigious amounts of stone, wood and rope, control some very passionate personalities, mobilize up to 300 workers, and try to move a megalith or construct a building in just a few weeks is no small feat. But it's only a pale imitation of the real thing. The ability to stage-manage a siege with a dozen trebuchets; to quarry, erect and transport massive shafts of stone; to build the lavish complex of buildings that comprised an imperial Roman bath – none of these ambitious ventures could have been achieved without a highly organized workforce and efficient systems of management.

They also require attention to the smallest detail, such as rope. Rope was essential to all our experiments, with the exception of the Roman bath, and in every case it caused problems. It would stretch. It would fray. It would break. One lesson we have learned is to pay a great deal of attention to rope.

By now I hope we have also learned to approach with caution any scheme involving rollers. Again and again, academic experts devise persuasive transport schemes whose key feature is the use of logs as pivots or wheels. As NOVA's teams on Easter Island and in Egypt discovered, rollers are overrated – and sometimes dangerous. They crush, or sometimes, with devastating results, they slip.

We have also learned that the simplest solution may well be the best. Looking at the elaborate wood frame and rigging that adorned the 25-ton obelisk as it lay stubbornly immobile at the end of its ramp, engineer Mark Whitby sighed, 'I'm starting to like the sandpit method better.' Meanwhile his rival and critic, stonemason Roger Hopkins, having twice demonstrated the simpler sandpit method with a much smaller replica of an obelisk, complained, 'If they ever give me a decent obelisk to work with, then we can do something. But no, I always end up in Dogpatch with the puniest little… you know what I mean.' In NOVA's final obelisk raising attempt, staged in Chelmsford, Massachusetts, the sandpit approach finally had its day.

Increasing our respect for the nameless engineers of ancient civilizations were the times that our modern technology fell short of the challenges they tackled routinely. Initially, for instance, the NOVA team wanted a much larger obelisk than the 25-ton replica we ultimately used. The quarry owner, Hamada Rashwan, managed to find a 66-foot section of granite that looked promising – about two-thirds the length of the tallest pharaonic obelisks – but it broke in half during quarrying, even though he was using modern methods. He then located a 43-foot piece in another quarry 130 miles away. But when he finally succeeded in loading it on to a truck, it was so heavy it blew out the vehicle's tyres. Finally he cut it down to 35 feet, about the size of one of the smaller ancient obelisks. That was as much as our modern equipment could handle.

All in all, we learned as much from our setbacks as from our successes. Experimental archaeology has its limits: proving that the ancients *might* have done something a certain way does not prove they *must* have done it that way. Would the Egyptians really have used a double-hulled boat to transport an obelisk over water, or rigging as complex as Whitby's to erect it? In the end, whether a method proves viable or not, the results of the experiment deepen our understanding of the accomplishments of ancient civilizations. To create exciting drama that brings an audience closer to appreciating the ingenuity, persistence and resourcefulness of the engineers of earlier times, while contributing to the body of archaeological knowledge, has been one of the many satisfying aspects of producing this series. But the greatest reward of making the series (which I privately call *Mysteries of Lost Youth*) is that it enables me to kindle in epic scale that purest pleasure of early childhood, engineering on the beach. I hope this book will do the same for its readers.

Michael Barnes
Executive Producer, *Mysteries of Lost Empires*

I

MEDIEVAL SIEGE

SCOTS, WHA HAE WI' WALLACE BLED,
SCOTS, WHAM BRUCE HAS AFTEN LED,
WELCOME TO YOUR GORY BED —
OR TO VICTORIE.

Robert Burns

It is the year 1304, and Edward Longshanks – known more formally as King Edward I of England – is campaigning against his unruly northern neighbours in Scotland. Most of the Scots surrendered early in the year, but one great castle remains in Scottish hands. Stirling stands high on a craggy outcrop 250 feet above the River Forth. This castle, and its gallant garrison under Sir William Oliphant, stands in the way of the final conquest that is Edward's dream.

The Scots had captured this castle from the English in 1299 by mounting a lengthy siege, which lasted nearly the whole year. Finally, when all their horses had been eaten and their supplies exhausted, the English defenders had surrendered. Five years later, impatient for revenge, Edward is in no mood to wait a year to exact it. The castle is strongly sited, and the fifty or so men within are well armed with crossbow and longbow. Close approach to the walls is dangerous, as Edward finds when a crossbow bolt lodges in his armour as he rides within range of the castle. A frontal assault is out of the question. What to do?

Industry is the better part of valour, he decides, and he settles down to watch as a horde of carpenters begin work on a dozen giant siege engines. One by one they are completed and set to work battering the castle gates or hurling stones against the walls. Some damage is done, but the men of the garrison retaliate with shots from their own engine, until eventually it breaks.

But in the English siege lines a monstrous machine is taking shape. Week after week it grows, and the sound of its name beats out on the air with each strike of the hammers. Warwolf, it is called; it is a name that will reverberate down through the ages. When finally it is completed, its very appearance is so terrifying that the castle's defenders immediately offer to surrender.

What was Warwolf? No firm evidence exists, but speculation centres on a mysterious type of catapult called the trebuchet. Long before the invention of the cannon, siege warfare from Bordeaux to Beijing was ruled by this ingenious form of heavy artillery, which harnessed gravity to fling gigantic missiles with great speed, accuracy and destructive power. Despite their central role in siege warfare, however, surprisingly little is known about how these ancient weapons were built and operated. How large were they? How accurately were they capable of firing, and with what frequency? How could such a machine remain out of range of a castle's defences and still muster the power to hurl missiles heavy enough to reduce stone walls to rubble?

No ancient weapon of this type has survived. An intact trebuchet was found at Liebvenmuhl in East Prussia in the 1890s when an old church was pulled down, but it was cut up for firewood. Today's knowledge is based on medieval accounts, which vary tremendously in accuracy, often including exaggerations and outright

lies. In the end, the only way to truly understand what the trebuchets were, how they worked, and what their capabilities were is to build one.

The idea is not new. In the nineteenth century Napoleon III directed the French army to attempt to reconstruct a trebuchet. The soldiers put together a machine 11 yards long, with a counterweight of almost 10,000 pounds. Using a preliminary, light counterweight, the machine evidently was able to throw a 24-pound cannonball a distance of about 175 yards. When Napoleon ordered the counterweight increased to 17,600 pounds, however, the whole thing collapsed. The records of even this semi-modern device are scanty, omitting such facts as the weight of the beam or the angle of discharge; there are no surviving plans.

The best reconstruction to date was accomplished in 1997 by a group of Virginia Military Institute cadets and about thirty members of the Timber Framers' Guild of America. They put together a 33-foot-tall machine using a counterweight of nearly 20,000 pounds to throw a 95-pound ball a distance of 700 feet (although the distance was measured downhill). It was an impressive accomplishment but fell far short of the ancient machine's legendary achievements.

In the summer of 1998, NOVA's producers decided to assemble a team to test the trebuchet in action. The goal: using medieval methods and materials, to build a machine capable of flinging a 250-pound ball at a 5-foot-thick stone wall 200 yards away – and destroying it. To double the challenge, the NOVA team decided to test not one but two competing designs. The crew of about forty members included a motley assortment of engineers, academic and amateur historians, and several dozen boisterous timber framers from both sides of the Atlantic.

After gathering in Glasgow in mid-October, the group set off on a three-hour bus trip through the highlands of Scotland, past Loch Lomond and over Rannoch Moor, until at the southern tip of Loch Ness they found the abbey at Fort Augustus, now converted into a bed and breakfast establishment. This spartan accommodation, distinguished by a lack of central heating, sparse furnishings and a single bathroom for every twenty guests, was to be their home for the duration of the two-week expedition.

Next morning, travelling north along the western side of the loch – 23 miles long and 900 feet deep – they reached Castle Urquhart, one of the great fortresses of Scotland, perched on a breathtaking peninsula overlooking the water. Here, in front of this twelfth-century castle, they began the attempt to go back into history and discover the truth about that awesome half-mythological creation: the trebuchet.

The trebuchet can be thought of as a cousin of the catapult. This better-known engine of war relied on torsion – the energy stored in twisted rope – to provide the force to propel its missiles into flight. Like the propeller of a toy plane, which is powered by a tightly wound rubber band, the throwing arm of the catapult was attached to ropes or sinews stretched between two poles, which were then twisted tightly. When the ropes were released, the arm sprang forward, releasing its missile.

It is doubtful whether the catapult of the ancient world was able to throw missiles as heavy as those later hurled by its lesser-known medieval cousin. Nonetheless, the historical record reverberates with accounts of the machine's impact. In the fourth century BC, as Alexander the Great marched from Macedonia through Greece, Egypt and India, the walls of formerly safe cities trembled, shook and shattered as heavy rocks came flying through the sky and pounded them into rubble. Combined with gigantic siege towers from which missiles cascaded on to the defenders and huge battering rams propelled by hundreds of men, Alexander's catapults pulverized the defences of the city-states in his path.

Through the centuries that followed, the pendulum of warfare swung violently from defence to offence and back again, as weapon begat counterweapon, keeping engineers and technicians happily employed.

Changes came quickly. In his first five years of conquest, Alexander broke through the walls of five major cities and a score of smaller ones. His private tutor, the renowned Aristotle, taught him that when rebuilding these cities, he should incorporate a maze of winding streets into their design. This, Aristotle assured him, would make it easier to defend his conquered cities against the army of future invaders who would surely be able to breach the walls, since 'catapults and other engines for the siege of cities have attained such a high degree of precision'.

By 200 BC Philo of Byzantium was writing a manual of warfare in which he specified that city walls should be built at least 15 feet thick to have a chance of standing up against a hail of catapult missiles, and that properly designed city fortifications should include moats and ditches to keep siege engines at least 200 feet away from the walls. The further the stones had to be flung, he reasoned, the lighter they would have to be and the less damage they could cause.

By this time offensive power provided an irresistible force. No matter how faithfully their rulers followed Philo's advice, it was no longer possible for isolated cities to build walls high or thick enough to keep out an army of attackers equipped with the monstrous siege engines. The reliance on great engines of warfare produced a class of engineers whose skill and education raised them above the general class of soldiers. Indeed, the very name of engineer stems from these weapons of war. They were commonly called 'engines' from *ingenium*, meaning an ingenious contrivance. Their builders came to be called *ingeniators*, which became engineers.

'Give me a lever and a place to stand and I will move the world,' Archimedes proclaimed. The lever found its ultimate expression in the trebuchet, invented in China around 480 BC – a century before Alexander began his march. Here the

Above *Long before the trebuchet made its way to Europe, Alexander the Great used torsion-powered catapults and other advanced siege weapons to conquer much of the known world. This detail from a Pompeiian mural shows Alexander at the Battle of Issus.*

Opposite *View of Urquhart Castle, on the shores of Loch Ness. This was the site of the 1998 NOVA trebuchet experiment.*

torsion type of siege machine was unknown. Just as the Rapanuians on Easter Island and ancient Egyptians used the lever to help move and raise enormous blocks of stone, Chinese engineers used it to achieve ever more destructive weapons of war.

In the earliest trebuchets, the lever took the form of a simple seesaw. As anyone who's played on a seesaw knows, two children of equal weight sitting equal distances from the fulcrum will balance each other. But put one child further from the centre and suddenly she seems to outweigh her partner.

The military technicians of ancient times realized that doubling either the child's weight or her distance from the fulcrum brings about a doubling of her effect on the seesaw. By combining a long arm on one side of the fulcrum with a short arm on the other, they could use a moderate weight to lift a much heavier one. From this insight it was a short step to the realization that the sudden application of a heavy weight to the short arm would raise a smaller weight on a longer arm very quickly – so quickly, in fact, that the smaller weight would fly off the seesaw into the air.

And thus was born the trebuchet. Although it originated in China, the name that has stuck is French in origin, interpreted variously as 'war machine' or 'balance', meaning a weighing device. The word 'trebuchet' does not signify a single, unique machine. In fact, experts still cannot agree on what exactly makes a trebuchet a trebuchet. Moreover, what we now call a trebuchet has been known by different names throughout the centuries, making it difficult to trace its evolution and use. It has been called *arrada, algarradas, ballista, biblia, biffa, blida, blide, catapulta, khattara, lapidisca, machina, machinella, machinetum, manga, manganellus, manganum, mango, mangonella, manjaniq, nangonels, petraria, tormentum, tormenta mangeranum, trabucium, tripantum* and *valsslongva*. It's not clear to which form of the weapon each of these terms corresponds, whether different names mean different weapons or not.

For example, *ballista* originally meant a torsion weapon which threw arrows, a sort of anchored crossbow. It later came to mean any kind of weapon firing projectiles. This is a constant source of confusion when trying to decipher the history of the weapons, a confusion which continues to the present day. It is often hard to distinguish in the sources machines that worked on the lever principle from those that relied on torsion.

The earliest trebuchet was a simple machine, consisting merely of a beam resting on a fulcrum. The fulcrum is supported on a high tower. The beam might be one spar or many lashed together, 6 to 9 yards long, and 1.5 to 2 feet thick. At the narrow end is a basket attached by iron wires that holds a missile weighing anywhere from just a few pounds to over a hundred, able to be hurled a hundred yards or more.

These first trebuchets, now known as traction trebuchets, used manpower instead of a heavy weight to provide the motive force. The weight of the projectile, housed in its basket, brings the throwing arm to the ground, leaving the lever arm pointing up into the air. From the end of that long arm dangle dozens or even hundreds of ropes. A muscular soldier takes hold of each rope, and on command they pull down simultaneously with all their might, flinging the projectile up into the air – towards the enemy, they hope, and not back down on their own heads.

Though the history of its journey from China across Asia is long lost, the traction trebuchet was used by Arabs as early as at the siege of Mecca in 683. In 708, a trebuchet known affectionately as 'The Bride' was deployed at the siege of Daybul, a machine so gigantic that contemporaries swore it took 500 men to operate it. Later weapons were said to require as many as 1200 men; even allowing for the possibility of exaggeration, the problem of organizing and synchronizing such a large force must have been nearly insurmountable.

One of the first written descriptions that survives is found in a treatise written for Saladin in 1187, while the fullest (though still imprecise) descriptions are to be found in the flowing Arabic of the *Kitab aniq fi al-manajahiq*, or *Elegant Book of Trebuchets*, written by Yusuf ibn Urunbugha al-Zaradkash in 1462. The translated Arabic names are picturesque: the machines are known as 'The Mother of Hairs of the Head', 'The Long-Haired One' and – a perennial favourite – 'The Witch from Whose Head the Ropes Hang Like Hair'. These refer to the traction machines, and are named according to their most obvious attributes, the ropes hanging from the lever arm.

The Arabs' adoption of the new technology seems to have been rapid: when Mohammed led his warriors against Ta'if in 630, it is said that he commanded a *manjaniq*, although this may have been a crossbow-type of weapon rather than a trebuchet. During the initial period of Arab conquests following the ascension of Mohammed, which lasted for about twenty-five years until it ended in the internal dissensions which accompanied the caliph Uthman, their siege practices were devoted more to ruses and treachery, since their siege machines were quite ineffective. But by the last few decades of that century they had adopted and learned to use the traction trebuchet to good effect.

From the Muslim world news of this marvellous machine spread into Europe. Trebuchets appeared first in Byzantium; from there the word spread to Sicily and onwards to Italy by the ninth century. By 873 the traction machine was being used by Norsemen in their siege of Angers, and at the Viking siege of Paris in 885. In 1134 one was used by the king of Denmark when he besieged Haraldsborg, although it was built and operated by Germans.

When armed with smooth, spherical stones the trebuchets were very reliable instruments of war. The challenge was to place them far enough from the defenders, beyond the effective range of their archers. If this could be accomplished, the only way of putting a trebuchet out of action was to make a sortie against it. This was easier said than done. Aside from the difficulty of opening the city gates to let out a raiding party without allowing the besiegers in, and the further difficulty of fighting their way to the machine, the defenders had the even more difficult job of rendering the machines useless.

How to do this? They couldn't cut the trebuchets to pieces since they were made of such large timbers. For the same reason it was hard to set them on fire: the attackers had not only to fight off the besiegers and take the weapon, but to hold it until the flames caught. During the Crusades, according to James I of Aragon, guards were mounted night and day to fight off sorties by bands of defenders who would dash out of the besieged city using faggots soaked in grease to burn the engines. At Balaguer they managed to set fire to the trebuchet's protective canopy – a comparatively thin wooden curtain built to shield its operators from arrows – but the engine itself was undamaged.

The only really practical way of dealing with these trebuchets was for the defenders to have some of their own, and to bombard the attackers with missiles as deadly as those sent against the city. And so the military history of the subsequent centuries is largely the story of the design and use of better and better trebuchets.

Soldiers haul away on a traction trebuchet in this depiction of the siege of Antioch in 1097. The pullers' ropes and the rings to which they are affixed are barely visible; the size of the projectile is obviously exaggerated.

The most significant advance was so radical as to amount to the invention of an altogether new machine. This was the development of the counterweight trebuchet, in which a heavy weight replaced the ropes and gravity replaced the muscle power used to pull on them. Picture once again a seesaw, this time carrying one very heavy and one very light person. Typically the heavy person sinks to the ground, holding the light one up high in the air. But if a group of people pull down on the light person, the situation is reversed: the heavy person sits up high while the lighter one is held down. At a signal, everyone holding the light person down lets go at once. The heavy person drops suddenly and the light person shoots up and is thrown off.

In the counterweight trebuchet the principle is the same, but the heavy person is replaced by a monstrously heavy weight and the light person by the missile to be thrown. A combination of muscle power and gears laboriously ratchets down the long throwing arm, raising the short lever arm with the heavy counterweight. Finally the throwing arm is locked into place and the missile placed in its basket. To fire, the lock is broken – by knocking out a locking pin or unhooking a hook – and the counterweight falls, hurling the missile skywards.

The apparatus seems simple but the exact mathematics is extremely complicated. The trajectory of the flung stone is determined by the length of the two arms of the seesaw and the weights of the missile and counterweight. But how could medieval engineers calculate the mass of the counterweight and the height of the throwing arm needed to propel a given missile a specific distance? In fact, how did they learn to design the machine so it flung the missile forward, not straight up, to fall back on their own heads?

As one historian put it, 'The engineer, Muslim or Christian, who constructed the first effective machine of this type deserves our unqualified respect.'

No one knows who that was. The machine appears to have originated somewhere in the Mediterranean area in the late twelfth century. The earliest unambiguous description from Europe is 1199, when the counterweight trebuchet was used in Italy. Its construction in England was well established by 1225, where its makers were called 'trebuchators'. Counterweight trebuchets are first reported in Islamic countries in 1248, at the siege of Hims. By 1291 the machine was being used by Muslims in great numbers at the siege of Acre. Returning the original compliment, details of the new machines passed back to China via Muslim engineers.

It may seem surprising that the traction trebuchet was known for perhaps a thousand years before the counterweight machine was invented. But the counterweight could not equal the pull of hundreds of men – a weight massive enough to exert the same amount of force would simply be too heavy. So the counterweight machines had a vastly smaller range than the traction trebuchets. Until the counterweight machine could operate beyond the range of enemy archers, it was a military failure.

Then someone came up with a clever idea: using a sling instead of a basket to hold the missile. The sling lies on a grooved rail on the ground parallel to the

This fifteenth-century German illustration from Konrad Kyeser's 'Bellefortis' is one of the clearest surviving depictions of a swinging-counterweight trebuchet. Note the length of the sling, placed in a grooved rail at the base of the machine, and the freely swinging basket that holds the counterweight.

throwing beam above it. When the weight falls and the beam lifts, the ropes that attach the sling to the end of the beam draw the sling along the rail before lifting it into the air. This allows the beam to pick up speed. When the sling lifts off, it swings upward in a nearly weightless extension of the beam, giving the missile high velocity at the moment of its discharge. In fact, the sling is actually accelerating faster than the beam, providing a whipping motion like that of a slingshot as the stone is released. The increased momentum generated by the use of the sling extended the range of the counterweight trebuchet. Once the correct proportions of sling length, counterweight mass, and ratio of lever arm to throwing arm were found by trial and error, it became the most feared weapon of medieval warfare.

The ultimate form of the trebuchet was the hinged, or swinging, counterweight machine. In this machine, the counterweight swings freely in a basket suspended from the short lever arm of the trebuchet. The trick involved in this final improvement was in allowing the counterweight to fall in a straight line rather than an arc.

The counterweight provides thrust by falling to the ground, and it does this through the force of gravity. But the most efficient way for the counterweight to respond to the force of gravity is by falling straight down, like Newton's apple. In the fixed counterweight machine, the weight must follow the curved path traced by the end of the lever arm as it rotates upon the fulcrum. But because the swinging counterweight is free to follow the optimal path, straight down, it is able to operate with more force.

How did medieval engineers figure this out hundreds of years before the discovery of gravity? By simple experimentation: they observed that weights dropping through a vertical distance had the greatest impact when they hit the ground. It was by piecing together such clues as this that Newton was able to construct the concept of gravity in the seventeenth century.

The swinging-counterweight trebuchets dominated siege warfare for several hundred years, continuing as the weapon of choice even after the discovery of explosive cannon. It was not until the fifteenth century that the innate supremacy of the cannon emerged and the trebuchet vanished beneath the sands of time.

Society in the Middle Ages was dominated by the lord's castle. Castles were at once military strongholds, administrative centres and noble residences. They provided a strong defence in case of war, offering protection to the townsfolk who huddled under their walls and the peasants who tilled the fields around. They also made an intimidating statement of power and authority. The name itself comes from the Latin *castellum*, the diminutive for *castrum*, a fortress.

The modern picture of medieval warfare, derived from novels such as those of Sir Walter Scott and from Hollywood movies, features armour-clad knights, axe-wielding peasants and hordes of archers clashing on the open field. The real face of medieval warfare – a long, dirty, boring siege – was less entertaining. Richard the Lion Heart, the greatest medieval warrior hero in folklore, fought only two or three battles in his entire career, but he was constantly involved in sieges, as both besieger and besieged.

Like Richard the Lion Heart before him, the English king Edward I generally avoided the risk of pitched battles. Instead he opted to surround the castles one by one and knock down their walls. Edward carried out some of his most effective sieges against the Scottish castles in an attempt to bring the Scots under his personal rule. A picture of the medieval siege has been given by an anonymous minstrel who accompanied Edward's campaign against the Scots in 1300: 'There were many rich caparisons embroidered on silks and satins; many a beautiful pennon fixed to a lance; and many a banner displayed. And afar off was the noise heard of the neighing of horses: mountains and valleys were everywhere covered with sumpter horses and waggons with provisions, and sacks of tents and pavilions. And the days were long and fine.'

When the army reached their target, Caerlaverock castle, they settled down for the siege. 'Then were the banners arranged, when one might observe many a warrior there exercising his horse; and there appeared three thousand brave men-at-arms; then might be seen gold and silver, and the noblest and best of all rich colours, so as entirely to illuminate the valley.' Tents were put up, 'and leaves, herbs, and flowers gathered in the woods, which were strewed within; and then our people took up their quarters'.

It's a magnificent spectacle, as much a party as a war. The king travelled in comfort. A description of a later campaign describes the king's tents as costing 500 pounds – a fortune in the currency of the day – and including porches, a four-posted chapel, and ten stables for the horses.

The rest of the army did not fare so well. Another contemporary writer, Jean le Bel, gives a more down-to-earth picture of the lives of the actual combatants in a campaign some twenty-seven years later against the same Scots. In words adapted by later writers and translated by British historian Michael Prestwich, the account reads in part:

> *Mounts and riders were tired out, yet we had to sleep in full armour, each of us holding his horse by the bridle since we had nothing to tie them to, since we left the carts which we could not have taken through this country... For the same reason, there were no oats or other fodder to give the horses and we ourselves had nothing to eat all that day and night except the loaves which they had tied behind their saddles... and these were all soiled and sodden with the horses' sweat. We had nothing to drink but the water of the river, except for some of the commanders who had brought bottles, and you can imagine that we were very thirsty after the heat of the day and all our exertions. And we had no fire or light at night, apart from a few lords who had brought torches on their sumpter horses.*

The party le Bel describes returned to Durham after only a few days. A properly provisioned city, huddled behind impregnable walls, could hold out for a year or more while the besiegers lived in misery and died of the myriad diseases that accompany overcrowding, dampness and lack of sanitation. Small wonder that a weapon that could breach the walls was regarded with awe, wonder and gratitude by the besieging army, and with dread by the city's inhabitants.

The siege of Stirling Castle in 1304 began like any other medieval siege. For three months, from May to July, Edward employed every kind of siege machine against its huge stone walls. The siege was a splendid spectacle. Edward's queen was present, and she and the ladies of the court had a special room with a fine bay window built in the town of Stirling, from which they could comfortably watch the proceedings. But despite all their efforts, all was in vain. The besiegers could not force the garrison to surrender.

Edward's hopes rested on building a huge new machine, a more formidable siege engine than any then known. He worked fifty carpenters for three months, building the great machine called Warwolf.

Despite the defenders' offer of surrender as soon as the beast was finished and ready for action, Edward was so worked up over their three-month intransigence and at having to spend so much money on the new war machine, that he refused to let them surrender with military honour. He insisted that they give themselves up to him unconditionally, which could have meant that he would have them disembowelled and hanged (in that order). When they came out, and a miserable sight they made, Edward's counsellors calmed him down. There were no executions. Instead the men were sent to various English prisons. Some conveniently expired there, though the commander of the garrison, William Oliphant, was released in 1308 to fight for the English against Robert Bruce. But before accepting any surrender, Edward couldn't restrain himself from trying out his new siege engine. The Warwolf bombarded the castle for a whole day, while the terrified garrison shielded themselves as best they could.

It couldn't have been much fun for them. Trebuchets by this time were hurling huge boulders weighing more than 300 pounds. Using counterweights of 10,000 to 30,000 pounds, they could throw such missiles more than 300 yards with considerable accuracy. It must have been a fearful experience to huddle behind the walls of the castle while these great stones crashed against them hour after hour.

At least, that is the historical theory, based almost entirely on reports of the effectiveness of the supposedly gigantic trebuchets Edward is reputed to have built. But it is hard to separate fact from exaggeration. Few descriptions of Warwolf and other magnificent siege engines have come down through the ages, and what remains is tantalizingly brief. Our state of knowledge is best summarized by a historian who wrote that so little is really known about details of trebuchet operation that 'the only way we may resolve how this artillery was actually used is by experimentation'.

The 1998 NOVA expedition sets out to construct two trebuchets, one using a fixed counterweight and the other with a swinging counterweight. Unlike previous reconstructions, these will be built on a scale large enough to test their capability to demolish a medieval castle wall. The designers of the fixed-counterweight machine are Hew Kennedy and Colonel Wayne Neel. A Shropshire landowner and medieval armour expert, Kennedy has been fascinated with trebuchets since childhood and has built several working machines from modern materials, amusing his neighbours by using them to hurl everything from dead horses to pianos. Neel, a professor of mechanical engineering at the Virginia Military Institute, oversaw the 1997 reconstruction of the 33-foot fixed-

Technical drawings prepared by designer and timber framer Ed Levin were used to guide the construction of NOVA's fixed-counterweight trebuchet (top) and swinging-counterweight trebuchet (bottom).

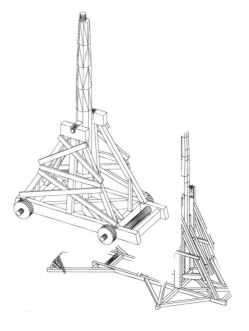

Right *The trebuchet depicted in this thirteenth-century manuscript, the* Cantigas de Santa Maria, *served as the basis for Wayne Neel's model. Note the wheels shown at the base of the trebuchet.*

Below *Levin's drawing of the base of the swinging-counterweight trebuchet closely mirrors the medieval drawing discovered by Renaud Beffeyte (opposite).*

Opposite Top *This fragment of a medieval manuscript by French engineer Villard de Honnecourt shows the base plan of a swinging-counterweight trebuchet and served as the basis for Beffeyte's design.*

Opposite Bottom *Another page from Villard's notebooks illustrates the use of animals to represent geometric relationships.*

weight trebuchet. He brings with him a working scale model based on an illustration found in a thirteenth-century Spanish manuscript, *Cantigas de Santa Maria.*

Hew Kennedy questions whether a correct trebuchet can be built from medieval drawings. The trebuchet in the Spanish manuscript, for instance, was not drawn to scale; people in the drawings are as tall as the machine.

'Today we accept that when you have a drawing for a project it's going to be accurate,' Kennedy says. 'That doesn't seem to be the case with these people. Their drawings indicate how it could be made, but that's all. This carpentry, for example, is quite impossible. I think that in these old drawings, one is probably chasing a fantasy.'

To lead the design and construction of the swinging-counterweight machine, the NOVA producers have hired Frenchman Renaud Beffeyte, a carpenter who has completed a seven-year course of study in '*compagnonnage*', restoring ancient religious building and castles. (When asked about his training, he replies only, 'These societies are extremely discreet, so nothing more can be said on this subject.') In 1984, Beffeyte was restoring the roof of a fourteenth-century castle whose owner was planning a medieval warfare museum and who hoped to create a full-scale trebuchet. Beffeyte immediately became interested and, after two full years of researching medieval archives, found the facsimile publication of the

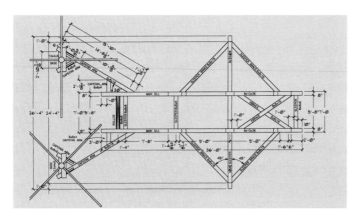

notebooks of a thirteenth-century engineer, Villard de Honnecourt, containing clues to the construction of a swinging-counterweight trebuchet. The manuscript included a rough drawing of the base of the trebuchet, but drawings of the side elevation were missing. There was also a brief written description of the box holding the counterweight.

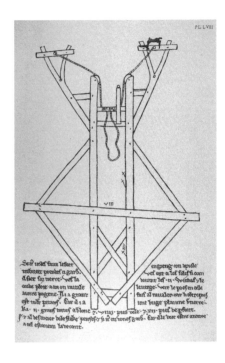

Like the *Cantigas de Santa Maria*, Villard's blueprint was not what an engineer would expect today. In those days even highly qualified carpenters were not expected to work from plans and drawings; moreover, their work was based on geometry and proportion rather than linear measurement and arithmetic calculation. Their manuscripts often used symbols, rather than figures or drawings, to illustrate geometrical relationships. Villard used stylized drawings of animals to remind carpenters of the proportions of one piece to another. For example, a rabbit represents 3 units, relative to a dog representing 5 units or a boar representing 7 units. But a rabbit might also represent a triangle, since a triangle has three sides.

Beffeyte managed to decipher the symbolic logic of the Villard manuscript, and over the following fifteen years built more than thirty trebuchets, although nothing nearly as big as the one planned here. He calculates that the machine diagrammed by Villard will be as high as a five-storey building.

'So you have these stone balls of two or three hundred pounds,' says Michael Prestwich, the British historian, as he inspects a prototype model of the Villard trebuchet. An expert on medieval warfare, he is one of the advisers to the NOVA team. 'You launch them off and they hit a wall. You think that repeated bashing like that will bring the wall down?'

Beffeyte is confident. 'I found an account where they shoot three hundred missiles in three days. Three hundred missiles in the same place on the same wall, and the wall was destroyed. That's what they did, and that's what we will do!'

His knowledge impresses everyone, and so does his good will. He is an especial favourite of the timber framers, an eclectic collection of forty or so free spirits who specialize in historical reconstructions. The project has drawn about thirty volunteer American timber framers under the leadership of Joel McCarty, president of the Timber Framers' Guild of America, along with about a

Beffeyte displays a wooden scale model of his swinging-counterweight trebuchet.

dozen of their English, French and German counterparts. Colourfully attired in flannel shirts, jeans and the occasional horned Viking cap, these skilled and dedicated artisans include frame designer Ed Levin, whose drawings help put Beffeyte's and Neel's visions into action.

'My first contact with the timber framers occurred one evening in a pub at Fort Augustus,' Beffeyte reflects later, 'where they were carrying on merrily. I knew immediately we would get along just fine. By the end of the evening I was even convinced my English had improved!'

On Monday, 19 October 1998, the timber framers begin to work outside Urquhart Castle, setting up a work site on the shore of Loch Ness. The castle, captured from the Scots by Edward I and later recaptured and used as a royal castle by Robert Bruce, is a vital part of Scottish history and a local tourist attraction. There is virtually no parking at the castle. To get there, Scottish guidebooks helpfully suggest that tourists walk to the castle from Drumnadrochit, the nearest village, which is several miles away. The timber framers, however, travel between the castle and the Fort Augustus Abbey, where they are staying, by bus. Already the weather is turning cold and damp; as volunteer Janice Wormington writes home via the Web, 'The showers leaked, the windows wept, the ceilings dripped and we learned to step over puddles on the cold tile floor.'

The first order of business Monday morning is to erect large tents – though not as large or sumptuous as those of Edward I – to protect their tools from the rain, sleet and snow, which mix with one another as they fall. English oak trees arrive by barge, and larch and fir from nearby forests are floated across the loch, much as they were in medieval days. By evening they have been unloaded and hauled into place. The largest oak log, 49 feet long and weighing nearly 6 tons, will serve as the throwing arm for the swinging-counterweight trebuchet.

The arm for the fixed-counterweight trebuchet will be much shorter – about 28 feet – but Kennedy and Neel have difficulty finding the right tree. They want to use a softer, lighter wood, like Scotch pine, since a lightweight arm may be more efficient. But Scotch pines aren't tall and thick enough. Kennedy has the idea of bundling four trees together to make the arm. He asks Joel McCarty to assemble the timber framers so he can explain his plan. The group dubiously agrees to hear him out.

Kennedy (left) and Neel debate the merits of Scotch pine and Douglas fir for use in the throwing arm of the fixed trebuchet.

'I'm not a timber framer or an archaeologist,' he apologizes in advance. 'But I thought it would be quite easy to make a beam for the fixed trebuchet out of several pieces of wood instead of one. Obviously if you make a hole here–' he sketches a diagram as he talks – 'probably the wood will break. But if you then take another piece of wood and put it there, strap these on, I would think it will work well enough.'

To the timber framers the idea of cutting a log into pieces only to tie it together again seems wrong. 'This is ludicrous!' calls a voice from the crowd.

'If you're worried about being ludicrous, what are you doing here at all?' Kennedy fires back playfully.

Someone suggests they use a Douglas fir, which grows in abundance in the vicinity. These grow so large that a single tree would do. Kennedy objects on the grounds that the tree was introduced to the area after the medieval period.

'The obvious thing,' says another timber framer, *sotto voce,* 'is to use the Douglas fir but not tell anyone what it is.' The team finally decides that Kennedy's composite arm is too complex and time-consuming to build; they will go with a single lever arm made of Douglas fir.

Another debate arises over whether the fixed-counterweight trebuchet should be equipped with wheels. Medieval illustrations occasionally show trebuchets with wheels, but wheels are difficult to fashion properly, and the group is in a race against time. Only two weeks have been planned for the expedition; they must fly home on 2 November, successful or not.

Scholars initially thought wheels were used to assist in transporting, emplacing and aiming the trebuchet. But when modern engineers began to reconstruct trebuchets, it became clear that the machines were so heavy that wheels wouldn't be of much use: there were few smooth roads in those days, and pushing the monstrous machines over hilly, rocky or muddy ground can't have been very practical. Instead, the trebuchets must have been built largely where they were to be used.

However, medieval engineers may have discovered that the wheels were able to absorb the recoil when the missile was fired. In fixed-weight machines there is both a horizontal and vertical component to the force of the counterweight as it falls to the ground along the arc of the lever arm. The horizontal component of the falling weight forces the machine to recoil in the opposite direction. The wheels allow the horizontal component of the falling weight to be absorbed in motion, as the trebuchet rolls a short distance, decreasing the shock to the system as the weight hits the ground. Otherwise, the structure would rear up into the air and slam back down, shaking itself to pieces. The use of wheels also meant that it was easy for soldiers to aim the machine. Once they found their target, they could fire again and again, bringing down a rain of destruction on the walls.

Unlike weapons designed for long sieges, the NOVA team's trebuchets are not likely to suffer repeated firings. Kennedy argues that the use of wheels as shock absorbers isn't really necessary for a weapon that will be fired only a few times. But Neel claims the wheels serve another purpose: they will enable the trebuchet to hurl missiles farther. This claim raises eyebrows.

'I shouldn't think it will work,' Kennedy warns. But Neel uses his scale model to demonstrate the effect.

First, Kennedy holds the trebuchet in place as it fires, negating the use of the wheels. They watch the missile fly, and Kennedy says, 'Right. Now let's try it with the wheels free to roll.'

And when they do, he is totally convinced. 'That's certainly better,' he admits. 'I would have thought that if you hold it firmly, such energy as it has would only be imparted to the throwing arm, so all the energy goes to the missile. But I ain't no scientist,' he shrugs.

The reason for the increased range becomes clear as they watch closely the workings of the model. The horizontal component of the falling counterweight actually pushes the wheeled trebuchet in the forward direction as it fires, adding its momentum to that of the sling. For the swinging counterweight, which falls straight down, there will be no such effect. It is decided to make wheels for Neel's machine but not for Beffeyte's. The NOVA machine will be the first reconstruction of a trebuchet with wheels.

Using a wooden scale model, Neel (left) demonstrates to Kennedy the use of wheels to extend the range of the fixed trebuchet.

While the timber framers are busy felling and hauling trees, a team of masons begins work constructing a replica of a thirteenth-century castle wall. They are members of Historic Scotland, an organization dedicated to preserving old buildings and making them available to the public. The structure, 25 feet long, 15 feet high and a full 5 feet thick at the base, is built to resemble the top 10 feet of a thirteenth-century castle wall, and uses the same sandstone and lime mortar masonry made of two parallel walls of sandstone and lime mortar. The gap between the inner and outer walls is filled with rubble, and the whole structure sealed off with a layer of stone and mortar. Like a real castle wall, it narrows at the top, with a crenellated row of blocks that may break off more easily under assault. The target wall also features a narrow opening through which defending archers might shoot, and a wooden balcony-like structure called a hoarding, which allows defenders at the top of the wall to drop rocks on attackers at the base.

Other stone-workers are kept busy chiselling away at the blocks of rock that will become the missiles. They must be smoothly rounded into an aerodynamic shape in order to fly long and true. Kennedy points out that objects of any shape can be thrown, but with a loss of efficiency due to air resistance. Throwing a piano through the air is a startling demonstration. 'If you throw a dead sow, which will weigh quite a bit more than a piano but is more aerodynamic in shape,' he says, 'it will go further. The aerodynamics are quite important.'

Still, the historical record is rife with all sorts of non-aerodynamic missiles. For ammunition the ancients used not only simple stone balls, but whatever could do damage to the walls of the city or castle – and the people behind them. Over the wall they pitched beehives, baskets of snakes or scorpions, cartloads of dung, shrapnel-like devices embedding small stones within clay balls, barrels of flammable pitch or oil, rotting animal carcasses, decapitated heads or the germ-laden bodies of plague victims.

Spies were also popular missiles. In the siege of Jerusalem, in 1099, according to a contemporary account, an Arab was captured while attempting to spy on the crusaders' siege machines. The soldiers bound him hand and foot, put him in the sling of a *petrera* and flung him towards Jerusalem. They missed, which irritated them greatly. (The chronicler does not report whether this was a source of solace to the Arab.) In 1345 the French besieging Auberoche caught a pageboy carrying a message for the English. They tied the letters around his neck and threw him into the city. It is reported that the knights inside 'were much astonished and discomfited when they saw him arrive'.

The NOVA team, however, decides to stick with stone balls.

Trebuchets hurled all kinds of missiles, from boulders to enemy soldiers' heads. This drawing based on a sketch by Leonardo da Vinci shows an engineer preparing to hurl a dead horse over the walls of a besieged town.

The sling is dipped in the loch and then hung from a tree to dry. The missile is placed in the sling to stretch the ropes and shape them properly.

The workers leave the thirteenth century each evening. Ed Levin later describes the experience in an article in the December 1998 issue of *Timber Framing* magazine:

> *Our modest tent city on the shores of Loch Ness can't have been much different from a medieval encampment of itinerant tradesmen gathered together to besiege a castle. Here the blacksmith strikes another lick as a new tool takes shape in the forge, there the foundrymen and women haul down the lift line of their timber derrick, tipping another lead casting out of the mold. With his helper cranking, the turner bears down on his lathe hog, the shavings fly and another axle begins to take shape, the framers tap, the flagmaker takes another stitch at her banner, the rigger calls time to his capstan crew as one more great baulk is hauled aloft, and all thread the muddy paths of the little village, swapping trade secrets and sharing quiet moments with fellow carpenters, carvers, cooks, engineers, framers, hewers, landscapers, masons, millwrights, riggers, seamstresses, smiths, sailors, stonecutters and weavers.*

On Thursday, four days into the project, the rain stops, the sun comes out, and the building of the two machines continues happily. The workers spend Friday touring nearby Stirling Castle, and by the weekend the cold muck of the Scottish autumn returns. The timber framers concentrate on putting together the base and wheels of the fixed-counterweight trebuchet.

Meanwhile design problems plague the swinging-counterweight machine. While Neel is using a pocket calculator to guide his work on the fixed-counterweight trebuchet, Beffeyte has limited himself to those tools available to a thirteenth-century worker: a compass and a square. Work on his machine is delayed while he works out the proper length of the throwing arm, upon which all other proportions depend.

The rains continue into the following week, alternating with lovely rainbows. 'You don't know what mud is until you experience a combination of clay soil, wet grass and straw, with rain added every day,' Janice Wormington writes home. The workers get a glimpse of what life was like for warriors in Scotland in the Middle Ages: their rooms in the abbey are cold and draughty, the showers cold with wet, dirty floors, and the electric clothes dryer is laughable. They begin to give up on washing their clothing. Nothing is ever dry.

A carpenter uses callipers to check proportions. Medieval carpentry was based on geometric relationships rather than linear measurements.

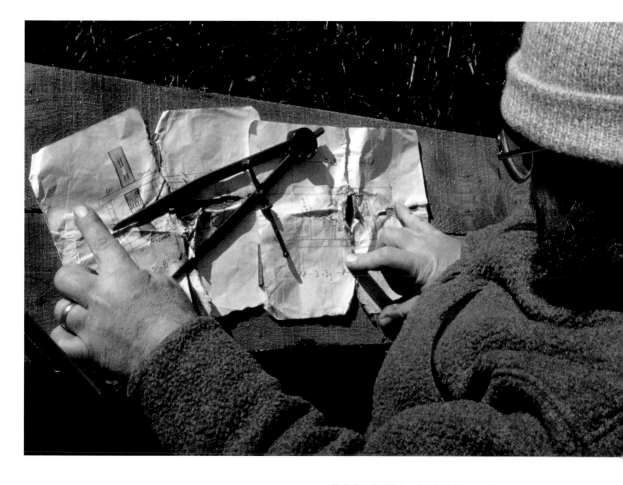

Workers haul on ropes to raise the second trestle into place on the fixed-weight trebuchet.

It doesn't matter: there isn't time for anything but building the two machines. The two allotted weeks seemed like plenty of time when they were planned, but now the days are slipping by and too little is being accomplished. Team members get up for breakfast at 6.30 am, board the bus at 7.15 for the 20-mile ride to the castle, work all morning, eat lunch standing in the tent to get out of the rain for a moment, then work till dark. Dinner is at 7 pm, after which they rest or wander down to the Lock Inn pub in the village.

On Thursday of the second week they begin to melt 7 tons of scrap lead to form the counterweight for the fixed machine. Unlike the swinging counterweight, which uses loose sand and stone, the fixed weight must be attached firmly to the lever arm. Kennedy is worried: 'It's a huge and quite difficult operation.'

'Lead melts easily with a wood fire,' Neel reassures him, pointing out that lead was commonly used in the Middle Ages as a standard roofing material. 'It'll work.'

So the lead is melted and poured into a 1000-pound half-octagon mould, cooled, derricked on to a trolley, then pushed uphill through the mud to the waiting trebuchet and bolted on to the lever arm. Kennedy and Neel are both right: it's a huge, difficult operation, but it works.

By Friday Beffeyte has worked out the proper length of his throwing arm and the proportions of the rest of the swinging-counterweight machine. With work progressing nicely on the base and components, he takes a few days off to attend to other concerns in France. While he is gone, a new problem arises.

He has devised a metal axle on which the throwing arm of the swinging-counterweight machine will turn. The fixed-weight trebuchet will use a wooden axle. But work has been backing up at the blacksmith's, and in Beffeyte's absence the team decides to build a wooden axle instead. But when the axle hole is drilled, it is made too large, seriously weakening the arm.

Some of the crew doubt the arm will hold under the stress of firing. Neel, however, is cautiously optimistic. 'It's on the verge. But I wouldn't want to use it for a lot of shots.' They decide to strap on wooden planks to strengthen the beam, attaching them with metal bands. This is not a simple procedure and causes some delay.

Meanwhile, the fixed-weight trebuchet actually begins to take shape. On Friday, the lever arm and the supporting sides are lifted into place to the

The fixed trebuchet is cocked, its 7-ton lead weight poised high in the air. When the trigger is released, the falling weight will hurl the missile at the other end of the throwing arm through the air.

accompaniment of wild cheering. And not a moment too soon: the deadline for departure is only four days away.

By Saturday a slight panic is setting in, and work continues by moonlight. The structure of the fixed-counterweight machine is in place, but the 7-ton weight is not yet attached. The axle of the other machine is repaired and the throwing arm is to be raised tomorrow. But the box for the counterweight is still not complete. Moreover, the continuing rains have turned the ground almost to quicksand; Beffeyte's machine is sinking into the mire, and anyone who stands too long in one place begins to sink too.

On Sunday the team decides to focus its efforts on the fixed-weight trebuchet in the hope that the timber framers will see at least one machine fire before they return home.

'There is a sense of real urgency and, I think, crisis about this,' says Prestwich, the historian.

'Chaos,' agrees Joel McCarty. 'The sun is going down, and we don't have a clue whether or not we'll finish.'

But finally the team is ready to lift the throwing arm of the fixed-weight trebuchet. They use a rudimentary lifting device used in medieval times, composed

of two trees assembled into an A-shaped frame, with their point of juncture set higher than the piece to be lifted. A pulley is attached at the point of juncture and used to haul the arm, weighted with 7 tons of lead, into position.

By mid afternoon the fixed machine is ready to fire. Teams of workers heave on the pulleys to cock the arm. As word spreads around the region, tourists come flocking to sit on the walls of Urquhart Castle and watch. Once in position, the arm is locked in place by the firing pin – and the team immediately faces another crisis as a metal strap that is part of the trigger mechanism begins to give way. It is not strong enough to hold the 7-ton weight. Working quickly, team members replace the strap with a length of chain.

Finally, the trebuchet is ready to fire. The 250-pound ball is set in the pouch of the sling, and all that remains is to pull the firing pin.

When trebuchets were being used, back in the Middle Ages, a constant danger was that the trajectory of the shot might not be quite what one intended. In 1205, when the Russians were besieging Livonia, they were just learning how to use the trebuchets. Much to the amusement of the city's defenders, the rocks they fired flew backwards onto their own troops. Another story tells how the Holy Virgin appeared to an artilleryman during the thirteenth-century siege of Seville,

The limestone missile begins its graceful arc through the air as the fixed-weight trebuchet is fired.

urging him to attend confession before the next day's firing. Luckily, he did, for he was killed when the rock he was firing fell backwards and landed on his head.

'Such examples help explain why modern researchers have so far not conducted practical experiments into the capabilities of lever artillery,' one historian notes dryly. Even Kennedy acknowledges that the ball 'has about a 50 per cent chance of going in the right direction', adding, 'It could go backwards into the lake. All these adjustments are not well known to us.'

With mounting trepidation, apprehension and above all a skyrocketing excitement, NOVA team members pull the firing pin. But with a truly pernicious sense of anticlimax, it won't come loose. More pullers are added, but it won't budge. Again and again they try.

Finally with one tremendous effort they pull it loose.

The 7-ton counterweight falls, pulling the missile backwards and slinging it up in its lovely arc. It releases perfectly and flies awesomely through the air. It doesn't hit the target but falls some 30 yards short – definitely a success for the first try.

'We'll shorten the length of the sling to release the boulder earlier, giving it a higher trajectory and hopefully a longer range,' says Neel. These adjustments are based on the mechanics of his scale model. Nobody knows if this will work.

It does – sort of. The second shot has the right range, but misses to the right by 2 feet as darkness falls and the day's work ends.

Monday, 2 November, is the NOVA team's last day. They mark the occasion with bagpipes; the timber framers don kilts.

In conjunction with the work on the fixed-counterweight machine, spurred by Beffeyte's disappointment, work has continued on the counterweight box and trigger mechanism of the swinging-counterweight trebuchet. 'We really don't want to let Renaud down,' says timber framer Marcus Brandt, who has thrown himself wholeheartedly into the medieval spirit of the enterprise. 'We really want to see this thing fly before we go.'

After the bagpipe concert the whole team pitches in to try to finish the swinging-counterweight machine before afternoon, when they must pack, grab something to eat, and catch the all-night bus to Gatwick airport.

The group works hard, but the job is truly monstrous. The trebuchet is as tall as a four-storey building, and it is slipping in the mud. If it slips when it fires, the falling weight will hit the treb's wooden scaffolding and destroy it.

In the meantime Kennedy, Neel and one of Neel's colleagues from VMI are working on reloading and re-aiming the fixed-counterweight machine. As expected, they find the wheels make it easier to shift the trebuchet to correct its aim. The engineers shift it one inch, and the command rings out: 'Fire in the hole!' This time the shot hits the wooden hoarding, but is too high for the wall itself.

'We're maybe a little high. We'll come down a little bit,' Neel says confidently, smiling now.

Using shear legs, ropes and pulleys, workers guide the arm of the swinging-counterweight trebuchet into place.

'Quite difficult, isn't it, these small adjustments,' Kennedy responds sceptically. For the next shot Neel lengthens the sling 6 inches to flatten the stone's orbit and shorten the range just a bit. He is afraid he may get only one more shot, and is determined to destroy the wall, so he makes one more 'small adjustment'. He replaces the 250-pound missile with a 300-pounder. Unfortunately the heavier ball overcompensates for the longer sling, and once again it falls short.

There is time for one final shot after all. This time they go back to the 250-pounder. The missile sails high through the air and hits dead centre on the archers' opening in the wall. Rubble flies through the air and into the mud. The team erupts with cheers and races to inspect the damage.

'It confirms what we came here to prove, doesn't it?' says Kennedy. 'A lovely hit, smack in the middle, and it smashed it and busted right through to the back. It's quite obvious that if you had one of these trebuchets and you have a castle like this and you've plenty of time to shoot it, you're going to knock it into a powder.'

Tuesday morning, Beffeyte returns to find that a handful of timber framers, Brandt among them, have stayed on, determined to fire the swinging-counterweight machine. He is afraid the iron straps reinforcing the lever arm may not be strong enough, so he decides to load the counterweight with only 4 tons of sand, one-third the planned capacity. The 300-pound ball is loaded into the sling, and everyone stands still, waiting for the signal to fire.

'Nobody knows quite what they're doing,' Kennedy comments. 'That's what makes it fun.'

For some, perhaps. Beffeyte steps back to calm himself by taking time to contemplate 'the beast', as he calls her.

'She was truly magnificent,' he recalls later, 'powerful, balanced, of noble breed. I sensed a real harmony and a mounting confidence. I silently thanked my operative ancestor, Villard de Honnecourt, and his little secrets of geometry.'

Stepping forward again, Beffeyte gives the signal to fire.

The weight falls, the sling flies out and up, the missile arcs into flight. But the 4 tons of sand loaded into the counterweight are not enough; the missile goes almost straight up and plops down in front of the machine.

They manage to load the machine again, using 6 tons of counterweight. This time the ball flies true but lands just a few yards short of the wall and to the right.

Above Taking a break from the construction, a worker pauses to look out from the basket he is building for the swinging-counterweight machine. The basket is large enough to hold 12 tons of sand.

Opposite Missiles hurled from the fixed-weight trebuchet lie in the mud before the damaged target wall.

They bend the hook that holds the sling, so that the sling will slip off sooner, releasing the ball into a higher arc. The ball flies far enough to reach the wall, but once again it misses, landing just to the right, as night falls.

The team is determined to try once more the next morning – the last chance to fire the second trebuchet. But they wake to snow, turning to rain. The wet, half-frozen ropes slip and fray as team members haul to lift the weight. Suddenly the rope snaps.

With redoubled determination, the workers splice the damaged ropes and manage to cock the trebuchet. But how to redirect its aim? The machine has sunk deep into the mud and is firmly anchored in position. Acting as artilleryman, Marcus Brandt suggests moving the sling channel a few inches to the left, in the hope that this will change the angle at which the sling releases the missile. Beffeyte, once again disconsolate, quite honestly doesn't give much credit to this idea, but no one else has any ideas at all, and so they try it.

The shot flies straight, but falls just 3 feet short of the wall.

Once more into the breach. They give the sling trough another nudge to the left, and the next shot flies through the wooden roof of the wall. They can't stop now. Beffeyte adjusts the hook again to make the sling release later, calculating that this will give the missile a flatter trajectory and so a shorter distance.

Direct hit! The ball smashes right into the already damaged centre. Now the bombardment begins. Subsequent shots 'turned the battlement into a red mist, with splintered wood and smashed stones everywhere', Brandt recalls later. 'One of the last shots hit the wall so squarely that it broke the ball into several pieces. You could see the tool marks of the ball imprinted in the shattered stones of the wall.'

By the end of the day eight balls have hit the wall, pretty well destroying it. No question now about the capabilities of these ancient trebuchets. 'That really proves that the trebuchet can break the wall,' M. Beffeyte exclaims, his excitement bringing back his strong French accent, 'and also that the trebuchet must be the Wolfwar – Warfwall – Warwolf!' he manages to get out, shaking his head.

'It's so difficult. We must change this name,' he laughs.

The project has provided the answer to several questions that have plagued historians for centuries. Were the trebuchets of legend such terrifying machines as contemporary accounts indicate? The answer is quite definitely yes. The great city of Acre in the Holy Land fell in 1291 after a battering from an incredible ninety-two trebuchets which destroyed the walls and towers, allowing the attackers to mount a frontal assault. At the siege of Aiguillon in south-west France in 1346 twelve machines were lined up, firing boulders at the ramparts. It's now clear that such a horde of trebuchets could well have reduced the walls to rubble and the defenders to terror.

Nonetheless, trebuchets were not invulnerable to conventional weapons. In the summer of 1999, the NOVA team conducted a second experiment to test this assumption. An archer armed with a medieval English longbow aimed its heavy war arrow at a dummy placed 200 yards away – the distance from which the fixed-counterweight trebuchet had fired. The arrow plunged straight through the dummy's belly. Any soldiers operating a trebuchet at that range would run the risk of assault from the archers defending its target, or else they would have to build a trebuchet powerful enough to operate accurately at even greater range – one larger still than the NOVA team's machines.

And why did the swinging-counterweight trebuchets systematically replace the fixed-weight machines? Theorists have argued that the new machines could throw heavier ammunition a longer distance, due to a more efficient use of gravity. But the NOVA experiments suggest that the main reason was probably logistical. The operators of a swinging-counterweight machine could dump anything heavy into the counterweight bucket: sand, stones, earth, rocks, whatever was to be found on the site. But the fixed-weight trebuchet needs a weight that can be affixed firmly to the lever arm. A rough mixture of sand and stones, for instance, would shift as the arm fell, tripping the machine over and destroying its aim, if not the machine itself. But only a dense metal like lead could be melted and moulded to the lever arm. If there were no convenient church roofs to strip, as there were at Stirling, the besieging army would have had to plan on carrying it along with them. Aside from the cost of the lead, its transportation must have been a nightmare to those leading a medieval pack train.

As the swinging-counterweight machine was perfected, it tended to supplant the fixed-weight trebuchets as the weapon of choice for besieging armies, and it retained its place of prominence for more than a hundred years. The last recorded instance of its use was in 1521, when the Spanish conquistador Cortés was besieging Tenochtitlan (now Mexico City). His trebuchet fired just one shot, which went straight up and came straight back down again, smashing the machine to pieces. Clearly the art of firing a trebuchet successfully had been lost by then, forgotten in the excitement over new technologies: gunpowder, cannons and explosive shells.

And the rest, as they say, is history.

2

PHARAOH'S
OBELISK

ONE HUNDRED AND FIFTY MILES UP THE NILE FROM THEBES,
ONCE THE CAPITAL OF EGYPT'S NEW KINGDOM, LIE THE ASWAN
QUARRIES. MOST OF THE GREAT MONUMENTS THAT
DISTINGUISHED THIS ANCIENT EMPIRE WERE MADE OF GRANITE,
AND THE PRIMARY SOURCE OF GRANITE WAS THE CLUSTER OF
QUARRIES JUST SOUTH OF THE TOWN OF ASWAN. ON A HOT
SPRING DAY, IN AN ANCIENT QUARRY JUST A FEW HUNDRED YARDS
FROM WHERE THE FAMOUS UNFINISHED OBELISK LIES, A GROUP
OF WORKERS SITS ATOP A LONG CHUNK OF GRANITE, SOME
TAPPING AT ITS ROUGH EDGES WITH ROUND STONES, WHILE
OTHERS CHISEL AWAY TO CREATE FINER DETAILS. THE AIR IS
TINGED WITH THE SCENT OF WOODSMOKE FROM SMALL FIRES THE
WORKERS BUILT TO TRY TO SOFTEN THE STONE AND EASE
ITS SCULPTING.

It is March 1999, but the scene looks much as it might have on a spring day in 1999 BC. For NOVA has assembled a team of engineers, stonemasons and archaeologists to conduct a series of experiments designed to show how the ancient Egyptians might have chiselled and carved the granite faces of the rocks they hewed into obelisks. But this is only the beginning. Using the same methods that the workers of the pharaohs Tuthmosis III, or Rameses or Hatshepsut, might have used, they will haul a 25-ton block of granite over land and transport a small model obelisk over water. Finally, they will face the greatest challenge of all: raising a replica of an obelisk to a permanent upright position without the aid of modern tools.

The modern Arabic word for obelisk is *messalah*, meaning 'large patching needle' or 'triangle'. The English word derives from the Greek *obeliskos*, or 'small spit'. No one knows the etymology of the ancient Egyptian word, *tekhenu* – but it was probably a bit more vainglorious than spit or needle. For obelisks were the great glory of Egypt's New Kingdom (1550-1075 BC).

The structure most commonly associated with ancient Egypt is the pyramid, and most people probably think of obelisks as contemporaries of these great tombs. In fact the pyramids were the work of Old Kingdom pharaohs, who reigned from about 2686 to 2181 BC. When the pyramids eventually became easy targets for gravediggers willing to risk the wrath of the pharaohs, the royal families eventually switched from entombment to burial in the famed Valley of the Kings. They built grandiose temples, and to adorn them they began to erect a new type of monument. Usually placed in pairs at the temple entrance, these shafts of polished stone seemed to reach up to the sky itself. Eventually, more than 1200 years after the great pyramids were built, obelisks attained a golden age of their own.

These great spires, each cut from a single chunk of granite, might rise as high as a hundred feet or more and weigh hundreds of tons. Carved on all four sides with elaborate hieroglyphics that proclaimed the glory of Pharaoh, the obelisks were designed to honour and appease the sun god, Amun-Ra. The Roman scholar Pliny the Elder observed that they resembled the sun's rays: bright shafts widening downward from a singular source up high. The tips, or pyramidions, were miniature pyramids covered with plates made of 'gold of the best of all countries' (as one pharaoh claimed).

Drawings and hieroglyphics on the walls of tombs give tantalizing clues about the obelisks. A Middle Kingdom tomb, for instance, shows a crowd of workers pulling a huge statue on a sledge. But just what sort of sledge could they have devised to transport such a great and precious weight as a giant obelisk over many miles? One drawing shows two obelisks being transported by boat. But it stretches the imagination to think what sort of boat the Egyptians could have designed to float such a giant. And then there is the greatest mystery of all: how were the ancients able to raise a 400-ton obelisk to a standing position, let alone a position so stable that it would stand for thousands of years?

NOVA's 1999 expedition isn't its first attempt to solve these puzzles. Four years earlier, NOVA commissioned archaeologists Mark Lehner and Roger

Hopkins to help with their initial effort to raise an obelisk. Lehner, an academic-looking Indiana Jones in safari hat and eyeglasses who is an Egyptologist at the Oriental Institute of the University of Chicago and the Harvard Semitic Museum, acted as consultant to a team attempting to raise a 40-ton replica of an obelisk. Hopkins, a stonemason with a bushy black beard who sported Hawaiian shirts and white scarf, tried a different method on a smaller replica. While Hopkins's method succeeded, the other team ran out of time and had to leave their stone leaning at an angle of 42 degrees. Now Lehner and Hopkins are finally back, along with engineer Mark Whitby, hero of NOVA's successful 1995 attempt to replicate a Stonehenge-style trilithon, to finish off the job.

Before undertaking this second-chance expedition, Lehner and Hopkins revisited some of the sites of Egypt's ancient glory, looking for clues that might give them the crucial edge in their quest. Strolling around the lofty pylon, colonnades and broad courts of the great temple of Luxor – the most visited temple in Egypt – they might have been any two tourists reflecting on the marvels of the pharaohs. Hopkins's visage showed the passage of the years: his beard gone, hair a bit greyer and thinner, he looked a bit like a muscular Beach Boy. Lehner looked like he just stepped out of the 1995 film: same hat, same glasses.

'What they did was absolutely incredible,' commented Hopkins, staring up at the obelisk of Rameses II, which shoots 82 feet up into the sky. A veteran of both NOVA's Stonehenge experiment and its earlier, successful effort to build a pyramid, Hopkins, like Lehner, is humbled by the challenges of building an obelisk. 'First just finding the stone – I mean, a single piece of stone as big as an obelisk is a real freak of nature,' he said. 'Then to quarry it out, in some cases removing a whole side of a mountain in order to remove the stone… Then to transport it to the river, get it down the Nile, off the barge, and into the temple without damaging it – I think by the time you get it to the site, the raising is almost anticlimactic.'

To sample the experience of creating an obelisk out of the good earth, the NOVA team finds itself at the Aswan quarry on this blistering March day, hacking away at granite with dolerite pounders the size and shape of six-inch-diameter cannon balls. Dolerite is a mineral harder than granite, found in abundance in the Eastern Desert. The only distraction from the feeling of being ancient quarrymen for the pharaoh is the sight of modern bulldozers in the background and the ferocious whine of saws cutting through granite. The hundreds of pieces of dolerite strewn about the quarries leave little doubt that they were among the ancient quarrymen's most common tools.

The NOVA team will not attempt the daunting task of hewing an obelisk from raw granite. But a few members spend twenty minutes or so getting a taste of the job. Holding the balls with both hands, the NOVA workers pound away patiently. Even after a few minutes, their fingers are scraped, wrists sore, and legs and backs aching.

Opposite Denys Stocks demonstrates how ancient workers used dolerite balls to pound the obelisk out of the earth.

For the ancient Egyptian granite workers, this was a way of life. To carve an obelisk, hundreds of quarrymen squatted shoulder to shoulder all day long for months in trenches that defined the shape of the colossal needle, in temperatures reaching 120 degrees F. To die on the job may not have been uncommon. Though the workers weren't exactly slaves, their labour was obligatory: being 'sent to the granite' was one punishment for prisoners.

Watching his team labour, Lehner muses, 'They didn't have Locke or Hobbes, no concept of individuality or freedom, no unions. It's hard to think it was fun.'

After carving out the top and sides of the obelisk, ancient workers faced the unenviable task of disengaging it from the mountain by lying on their sides in the trenches and pounding out the rock beneath its underbelly. Finally, workers on opposite sides would come within a few inches of each other, leaving the obelisk supported only by an elongated sort of keel (much like the Easter Island *moai* at a similar stage – see Chapter 3). The workers would scamper out of their trenches, and the obelisk would be liberated from the earth as leverers snapped it off its keel, leaving a spine of rock protruding from the quarry.

Cracked in several places, the Unfinished Obelisk of Aswan remains tethered to the granite from which it was carved. Like other unfinished obelisks, it provides important clues to the way obelisks were made.

The NOVA team, however, has neither the time nor the resources to quarry an obelisk in the style of the pharaohs. They need an obelisk fast. In 1999, as in 1995, they are working in the quarry of Hamada Rashwan, known locally as the 'king of granite'. Confident and loquacious, Rashwan dresses in a sports jacket and sweater even in the stifling heat. NOVA has commissioned him to provide a large obelisk for the main raising. (A smaller replica obelisk, left over from the 1995 expedition, will be used for side experiments.)

There is no question of providing an obelisk as large as the great ones of old. After several false starts, Rashwan locates a 43-foot piece in a quarry 130 miles to the south, in what was once the ancient land of Nubia. After quarrying, it takes sixteen hours to load it on to a truck for transport. The great weight proves too much, blowing out several of the truck's tyres. So Hamada cuts the stone down to 35 feet. What they have now is only a third the size of the largest ancient obelisks, but equal to some of the smaller ones. Successfully raising it, then, will show how at least some of the ancient monoliths might have been erected.

Rashwan was not the first to run into problems quarrying a large obelisk. The most famous example is the great Unfinished Obelisk of Aswan. Measuring 137 feet long and nearly 14 feet wide, it lies still tethered to the mountainside. If it were freestanding, it would weigh about 1100 tons. Much of what archaeologists know about how obelisks were made comes from the study of this massive work in progress.

No one knows which pharaoh commissioned this obelisk. The pharaohs were not shy about proclaiming their prodigious achievements, but it's not surprising that none would admit to this failure. It may have been the work of the great female pharaoh Hatshepsut, around 1500 BC, who erected some of the largest obelisks in ancient Egypt. Others say it may have been the work of her stepson, half-nephew and successor, Tuthmosis III, who inherited his stepmother's passion for obelisks.

Tuthmosis III may also have planned to salvage the stone: the outline of a smaller obelisk is still barely visible on its upper face just after sunrise or before sunset. The outline has the same dimensions as the largest surviving obelisk he erected, which now stands in Rome's Piazza San Giovanni in Laterano. At 105 feet high and 455 tons, it is the largest obelisk still in existence. Its hieroglyphs explain that unlike most obelisks, which stand in pairs, this enormous monument was meant to stand alone at the centre axis of the temple of Karnak, the national shrine of the New Kingdom. Six other obelisks commissioned by Tuthmosis III were erected in the temple.

In the winter of 1921, Sultan Fuad of Egypt visited the Unfinished Obelisk, which was then half buried, and suggested

The Lateran obelisk in Rome is the tallest standing obelisk in the world.

that the whole stone be cleared for the purpose of study. Reginald Engelbach, a British engineer and archaeologist who directed the excavation, wrote the definitive monograph on the work, *The Aswan Obelisk, with Some Remarks on the Ancient Engineering*. 'A study of the Aswan Obelisk,' he wrote, 'enables the visitor to look with different eyes on the finished monuments, and to realize, not only the immense labour expended in transporting the giant blocks and the years of tedious extraction of stone in the quarries, but the heartbreaking failures which must sometimes have driven the old engineers to the verge of despair before a perfect monument could be presented by the king to his god.'

The despair of the engineers couldn't have been greater than that of the quarrymen. After months, or even years, of hellish work, a fissure appeared near the base of the great slab. The engineers scaled back the project and the quarrymen resumed their labours, but to no avail. Some time later, another crack appeared, then another. Finally a fissure near the centre rendered the entire project unfeasible and the obelisk was abandoned to the centuries.

'It must have been galling beyond words to the Egyptians,' wrote Engelbach, 'to abandon it after all the time and trouble they had expended, but today we are grateful for their failure, as it teaches us more about their methods than any monument in Egypt.'

Other unfinished obelisks have revealed clues regarding their polishing and decoration. For instance, one that broke on the way out of the quarry is already polished and inscribed on three sides, proving that at least in certain cases fine, detailed work was done before the obelisk was removed from the quarry. Pharaohs are also known to have added hieroglyphs or erased images after the obelisks were erected.

At least one Egyptologist has suggested a method of polishing that began with pressing flat planes covered with red ochre against the surface. Any projecting areas would turn red and could then be pounded down with dolerite balls. After that craftsmen probably used a series of treatments to get the fine polish. In a 1995 NOVA experiment, Hopkins showed how they might have done it, using a flat stone to rub coarse sand, then a finer sandstone, and finally a very finely grained limestone against the granite surface to polish it, washing the resulting dust away between rounds.

After polishing, the obelisk was ready for inscription. Most obelisks carry, along with other information, long-winded declarations of the glory of Pharaoh. The hieroglyphs might also tell of military victories, such as those of Tuthmosis III. After returning from successful campaigns in Asia, he erected two obelisks at Karnak, proclaiming himself 'the lord of victory, who subdues every [land] and who establishes his frontier at the beginning of the earth [the extreme south] and at the marshland up to Naharina [in the north]'.

At least Tuthmosis's braggadocio was based on actual conquests. Most pharaohs felt no need to conquer anyone before bragging about it. Rameses II, for example, hardly deserved to be called 'the one who defeats the land of Asia, who vanquishes the Nine Bows, who makes the foreign lands as if they were not'.

Opposite Carved head of Rameses II from the temple at Luxor.

Although he personally commanded a great battle in Syria against the Hittites, it ended in a draw. Only his mother (and perhaps his fearful subjects) might have believed that 'his power is like that of Monthu [the god of war], the bull who tramples the foreign lands and kills the rebels'. In some cases, Rameses II, better known as Rameses the Great, creator of many of Egypt's grandest monuments, merely had his cartouche chiselled into the granite of earlier pharaohs' obelisks. (When one of his obelisks was removed to France in 1831, it was discovered that he had had his name carved into the base, where no one could see it, to guard against any future pharaoh repeating his own brand of chicanery.)

The tales found on obelisks, though, were more than the mere boasting of politicians. The pharaohs were attempting to ensure that they would partake of the power of Amun-Ra in this world and the next, and that their glory would endure

Above Painting from Rekmires' tomb at Thebes showing granite sculptors using stone tools.

in the next world. Obelisks were dedicated to the sun god and other gods, and the kings would lay offerings at their pedestals. The preservation of the pharaoh's *ka*, his life force, would ensure a smooth passage to the underworld. 'If I could sum it up in one word,' says Lehner, 'I would say the obelisk stood for resurrection.'

As for Hopkins, he focuses on the material rather than the metaphysical, marvelling at what he calls 'some of the finest stone sculpture work in history'. As impressive as the imprinting of hieroglyphics, he says, was the ancient Egyptians' cutting and drilling of granite. In the Egyptian Museum in Cairo, for instance, one can find drill holes on the granite sarcophagus of a Twenty-first Dynasty pharaoh from about 1000 BC. Rectangular holes on the four corners were meant to hold the lid in place. On the side, circular holes 8 inches in diameter were made for decoration. Another coffin, excavated from a Fourth Dynasty (*circa* 2600 BC) private tomb east of the Great Pyramid, displays deep, clean slices made centuries before the introduction of even iron tools.

'Even with modern tools – stone chisels and diamond wheels – we would have a tough time doing such fine work in granite,' he says.

How, then, did they do it twenty or even forty centuries ago? NOVA brought Denys Stocks, an ancient-tools specialist who has been re-creating Egyptian tools for more than twenty years, to investigate how the pharaohs' craftsmen might have both sawed and drilled granite. One rare scene drawn in an ancient tomb gives a clue. Craftsmen are pictured putting in detailed work on a granite statue with stone tools, probably quartzite and sandstone. Copper and bronze, the hardest metals at their disposal, would have been useless against granite – if used in a conventional way.

Stocks, with white hair and a stoic demeanour, demonstrates an ingenious method that would have been available to the Egyptians. First he chips out a rough groove. Then, before applying a copper saw, he sprinkles sand into the groove. Common Egyptian sand contains quartz crystals which are hard enough, when dragged by the saw, to cut through the granite. 'We're going to let the sand do the cutting,' Stocks says, as he and Hopkins begin to work the saw from either end.

'Now, Denys,' says Lehner, trying to get a rise out of him, 'will we see any progress in our lifetime?'

'Yes,' Stocks replies calmly, 'if you came back in an hour's time, you would see about a 4-millimetre cut down into the stone.'

Sure enough, the sand-saw method proves viable. A few days later, Stocks's stone boasts an impressive knife-clean slice.

While other team members take turns working the saw, Stocks demonstrates a similar method of drilling holes with a copper bow drill. As the drill turns and the sand sprinkled on the surface of the rock begins to cut into it, granite dust begins to accumulate in the shallow scratch. This bothers Hopkins.

'You know, without a steady stream of water here, you are not getting rid of the old powder, which is just interfering with the drill going down,' he points out.

'No,' Stocks answers, 'the sand acts just like a fluid in this case.'

Hopkins persists: 'I've done this for twenty-five years. I've done it dry and I've done it wet, and believe me, wet is much better.'

Stocks responds with a stubborn scowl.

'This water,' Lehner tries to mediate, 'is a very controversial thing between all the experts in ancient granite drilling – that is to say, the two of you. Anyway, I think by about our tenth sarcophagus we would know the answer to which one is better.'

Hopkins decides to try his own side experiment with a saw and water, while someone else takes his place working Stocks's drill. In the end, both methods produce impressively neat marks. After boring down several inches, Stocks carefully pops out a cylinder of granite, leaving behind a beautiful hole nearly identical to those on the ancient sarcophagi. Stocks later determines that the same amount of rock is displaced by either method of sawing, indicating that in fact the water was not necessary. He also finds that the dust produced by these methods – a combination of granite, sand and copper particles – forms the main ingredients in faience, the deep blue glaze commonly used in ancient Egypt.

Denys Stocks and Roger Hopkins demonstrate the use of a copper saw and sand to cut granite. Hopkins sprinkles sand into the groove while workers use the saw to drag the crystals through.

After the Egyptians carved an obelisk from the mountain, cut it, polished it, inscribed it on three sides and finally dislodged it, the hard work began. The monument had to be transported from the quarry to the great temples near Thebes, some 150 miles to the north. To drag a hundred-ton stone that far over land would have been impossible. Luckily, the Egyptians had a magnificent natural freeway at their disposal for almost the entire trip: the mighty Nile river. Still, just to get the obelisk to the river was a daunting task. Building a boat to carry such a monolith was one of the great challenges of the age. No one knows exactly how the Egyptians accomplished these tasks. There are but a few clues from ancient drawings and scripts. The rest the NOVA team hope to deduce by attempting it themselves.

The Aswan quarries, where most of the obelisks were produced, lie within a few hundred yards of the Nile. The route is mostly downhill, and the Egyptians built a series of wide paths on which to pull their obelisks. But there was still the challenge of moving the huge structures without damaging them – and controlling the descent.

For other obelisks distance became a factor. Obelisks made of beautiful red quartzite were carved at the Gebel Simaan quarry, located on a plateau several miles west of Aswan. There, mostly buried in thirty-three centuries of sandstorms, lies another unfinished obelisk, its pyramidion and part of its shaft peeking out. Pharaoh Seti I commissioned this obelisk near the beginning of the thirteenth century BC. Visitors who are willing to endure the gruelling camel ride – the only way to get there – can still make out Seti I's hieroglyphics.

Leading towards Aswan from Gebel Simaan, across a stunning vista of windswept sand dunes and occasional boulders, lies the faint remnant of an ancient road. Thirty-five to forty feet wide, paved with rock-thickened sand, this is what remains of the monstrous migrations of obelisks to the water. Reginald Engelbach suggested two ways that the obelisks might have travelled this road. One was to roll them the way loggers roll trees. The road is wide enough to accommodate most of the known red quartzite obelisks in this fashion. But without a protective frame this method would damage the obelisk. And it would be very difficult to construct a frame suitable for rolling. Instead, most experts today think that Engelbach's other suggestion is more valid: that the Egyptians pulled the obelisks along the road on a wooden sledge, possibly with rollers underneath. The wide road would still have been necessary to accommodate the crowd of pullers.

This drawing, based on a relief in Djehutihotep's tomb, shows a large statue being hauled on a sledge. It is one of the key pieces of evidence suggesting how obelisks were transported over land.

One crucial piece of evidence supports this logic. On the wall of one Middle Kingdom tomb, from the twentieth century BC, there is a drawing of a great statue of the noble Djehutihotep being transported. The statue sits on a sledge, and 172 men pull on four ropes attached to the sledge. One man stands on the statue's feet, pouring what may have been a lubricant over the sledge runners, and another man, apparently the foreman, is perched on Djehutihotep's knees, shouting out the pulling cadence. Egyptologists have estimated the weight of the statue at 57 tons. The scene is the only one discovered in Egypt showing how massive weights might have been transported over land. However, archaeologists

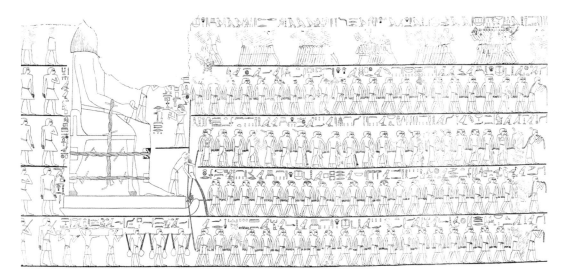

have also found clay beds with wooden sleepers laid out like railroad ties, which might have been used for hauling.

The challenge for the ancient Egyptians was similar to that faced by the Rapanui of Easter Island many centuries later: to design and build a wooden sledge that would allow a crew to drag a huge stone several miles in the most efficient manner possible. The only difference was one of scale: Easter Island's *moai* weighed up to 80 tons, while the obelisks were as heavy as 500 tons. No wonder the hieroglyph for 'sledge' was used to write the word for 'marvel'.

In 1995, Lehner and Hopkins had tried putting the stone on wooden rollers. But the NOVA team made the same sobering discovery as the NOVA scientists on Easter Island in 1998: 'Rollers crush,' as Mark Whitby succinctly put it, in his confident, clipped English accent.

In 1999, in Rashwan's quarry, the new NOVA team tries land transport again. Rais Abd el-Aleem, a stooped, thin man with a hoarse voice, serves as the foreman for the sledge project. Although he normally uses trucks and cranes, he takes to the challenge of experimental archaeology. He builds a track of wooden crossbeams set out like railroad ties. Initially, the NOVA team had suggested that the beams be buried in tufla, a fine clay, which could be moistened and made slippery. For reasons known only to himself, however, Abd el-Aleem insisted on setting the crossbeams on top of the ground and applying tallow, or animal fat, to the wood for lubrication.

Lehner, Hopkins and Whitby watch as Abd el-Aleem assembles his team of pullers. He has already used his trusty crane to load a 25-ton block of granite on to the sledge. (The obelisk is not ready yet.) The scientists are impressed with the design.

'I would reckon that a hundred people are going to shift this thing easily,' says Whitby. 'You could probably cut right back down to fifty once it's moving.'

Hopkins agrees: 'I would think seventy-five would be sufficient.'

Abd el-Aleem, a white sash tied around his head, is finally ready to go. He has sixty men arranged on four ropes. 'Hela hop!' he shouts. The words have no meaning in Arabic, and no one knows the source of this commonly used working chant; it is possible that it is descended from the ancient Egyptian tongue. The pullers heave on the ropes. Nothing. Reserves are brought in; now there are a hundred men pulling. Still the rock will not budge.

Hopkins approaches the sledge. 'What did they do, cement this thing down?' He pleads for the use of levers. Within minutes a number of the men are manning wooden levers as thick as telephone poles. At last, assailed by the hundred men and the levers, the rock's inertia gives way and the sledge begins to creak forward. It crawls 2 feet down the track – and then a rope breaks and a line of men topples to the ground like dominoes.

At lunch, there is but one topic of conversation. Hopkins wants more levers and more levering points. Whitby bemoans the lack of communication: the mix of American and Egyptian workers seems to have led to confusion, and it's hard to hear Abd el-Aleem's raspy voice. Lehner agrees, saying the pullers need to get their rhythm in sync.

'The problem is we have a lack of people in charge,' he says. 'The power and expertise are diffusing through the crew.'

'Yeah,' nods Whitby. 'Maybe Roger can get something going.'

After lunch, Abd el-Aleem manages to round up more than 200 pullers and leverers. Hopkins, obviously eager to get his chance at the reins, sidles over to Lehner and Whitby. 'You want me to take over?' he asks.

'Please,' says Whitby.

Hopkins hops right on top of the block, like Djehutihotep's foreman, and begins to whip the pullers into a frenzy with a rhythmic chant. Time and time again they heave on the ropes, pulling the sledge a few inches each time. Several times a rope breaks, and work stops while workers retie them. With the reddening sun dipping into the Nile, Hopkins raises his voice again: 'This is our last chance! *Allah akbar!* [God is great!]'

The sledge moves, and this time it doesn't stop for a good ten feet. Twenty feet in all for the day. Perhaps it wouldn't have been good enough to spare Djehutihotep's workers a flogging, but for this team it is a triumph. The men let out a great whoop and carry Hopkins off on their shoulders, parading him around like a Super Bowl coach.

Hopkins stands atop the 25-ton block of granite, urging the pulling crew on as they drag the sledge across the track of lubricated rollers.

Whitby, however, remains sober. Off to one side, he is ruminating about a problem that will return to plague him in the week to come. He is worried about the ropes.

Hundreds of obelisks stood in ancient Egypt, more than fifty of them higher than 30 feet. Many of them were obliterated by later pharaohs; others crumbled over the centuries. Now only six of that stature remain; of these, only three (all in Luxor) have never been moved. Seventeen, however, still exist outside Egypt. Of these, thirteen stand in Rome, once called the City of Obelisks.

After Augustus Caesar defeated Mark Antony and Cleopatra at the battle of Actium in 30 BC, the former heart of civilization became little more than a granary for the Roman Empire. But the Romans were well aware of their protectorate's grandiose history, and they revered the glory of the pharaohs. They even portrayed their emperors in pharaonic style on their temple walls.

Around the time of Christ, Caesar Augustus visited Egypt and was awed by the greatest obelisk of them all. Probably the work of Tuthmosis III, it stood 105 feet high: 455 tons of red granite, from the same Aswan quarry as the Unfinished Obelisk. He was sorely tempted to remove it to Rome — what greater monument to his own glory? — but his advisers finally convinced him that even Caesar's armies could not safely transport such a behemoth. He may also have been afraid of incurring the wrath of the gods.

Three centuries later, the emperor Constantine was hampered by no such religious scruples. He had the great obelisk pulled down — severely damaging its base and pedestal — and dragged to Alexandria to await the construction of a barge that would carry it to his new capital, Constantinople. Unfortunately, Constantine died in AD 337, before the barge could be built, and his son Constantius ordered the obelisk rerouted to Rome. After a long journey, it was finally erected in 357 at the Circus Maximus as a tribute, strangely enough, to the ascendance of Christianity.

Twelve centuries later, Tuthmosis's spire lay in pieces, buried 23 feet below the fields that had grown over the great Circus. Pope Sixtus V had it reassembled and erected in the Piazza San Giovanni in Laterano on 3 August 1588, and there the so-called Lateran obelisk still stands.

For the most part, though, ancient Egypt held little interest for the outside world until the late eighteenth century AD. The person responsible for rekindling interest in Egypt was yet another imperialist conqueror. When Napoleon Bonaparte sailed to Egypt in 1798 to begin a three-year campaign against British and Turkish forces there, his retinue included a group of scholars. Napoleon fell to the British, but his scholars fared better. They produced an impressive tome, *Description de l'Egypte*, documenting the appearance and customs of Egypt's major cities and towns as well as presenting a complete catalogue of all the extant ancient monuments. They even copied the hieroglyphic texts on the monuments, although they had no way of deciphering them.

Suddenly, Egypt was all the vogue. Archaeologists began unearthing treasure after treasure, and the emissaries of many countries began collecting objects for their embassies and home governments. Then in 1822 Thomas Young, a British physicist, and Jean François Champollion, a French Egyptologist, announced that they had deciphered the Rosetta Stone. This slab of black basalt dating from 196 BC carries an inscription praising the Greek ruler of Egypt, Ptolemy V, written three times – once in Greek, once in demotic script, and once in hieroglyphics. Suddenly the vast record of the pharaohs and their monuments emerged like a mountainscape after a storm.

It was the birth of modern Egyptology, and it accelerated the new demand for Egyptian relics. The governments of England and France, in particular, decided that obelisks would make fine ornaments for London and Paris, glorifying the capitals of the great modern empires as they had the old. It may be surprising now, but they had no trouble gaining permission to remove the priceless objects. Mohammed Ali, the viceroy of the Turkish sultan, who was the effective ruler of Egypt at the time, simply arranged who would get which as though dividing candies among covetous siblings.

Obelisk adoption, however, was more easily approved than accomplished. France and England managed to carry away only one obelisk each, and they made their choices based mainly on which might most easily be removed.

Visitors today to the Place de la Concorde in Paris take the Metro to station Concorde. Standing before them as they ascend to the street is a 75-foot, 227-ton obelisk created for Rameses the Great. Some onlookers may believe that the marvel of seeing this great pharaonic spire in Paris is the result of the famous words of Josephine to her husband Napoleon as he departed for Egypt: 'If you go to Thebes, do send me a little obelisk.' The words are probably apocryphal, however. Neither Josephine nor most other people were lusting for obelisks before Napoleon and his scholars visited Egypt. And in any case, Rameses's obelisk was brought to France to satisfy the wishes not of Napoleon or his wife, but of King Louis XVIII, following the restoration of the monarchy in 1814.

The hero – or the villain, depending on your point of view – of this attempt to transport Rameses's obelisk, however, was a naval engineer, Apollinaire le Bas. He was chosen by the Ministry of the Navy to bring back the obelisk adorning the western side of the entrance to the great temple of Luxor. On 15 April 1831, le Bas sailed from Toulon on the *Louxor*, which had been years in the construction for the purpose of transporting obelisks down the Nile, across the Mediterranean and up the Seine to Paris.

On 8 June le Bas met Mohammed Ali in Alexandria and secured the full co-operation of the pasha, who seemed as eager as ever to slake all foreign thirst for his country's treasures. A few days later, le Bas left Alexandria and made the long journey first to Cairo and then up the Nile to Luxor. There, he found that the western obelisk was cracked a third of the way up its shaft. Furthermore, the entire Temple of Luxor was surrounded by houses and streets; unconcerned with the history of the place, the local population had built their current town right on top of the temple.

Le Bas got to work negotiating. He paid for the right to remove thirty houses and make a path for his obelisk. Then, in the 120-degree summer heat, his workmen began to clear the great path; his carpenters began to build scaffolding of soft pine around the obelisk; and his sailors built a ramp to load it on to their ship. From 23 October to 16 November, 190 men worked to lower the obelisk. When they finally had it prostrate, they were the first to discover that Rameses had had his name engraved on the bottom to foil usurpers.

A month later, they had the obelisk on board the *Louxor*. 'After four and a half months of fears and worries the problem is solved!' wrote le Bas. However, it was ten months more before he arrived in Paris with Rameses's obelisk and erected

it before 200,000 spectators. Le Bas received a large honorarium and silver and bronze medals from King Louis-Philippe I – Louis XVIII having died before his wish for an obelisk could be fulfilled.

Le Bas and his workmen remove the obelisk from the Temple of Luxor.

Back in Luxor, some locals happily counted their bribes and tips. Others, however, muttered about 'the work of devils'. The French had removed one half of the only pair of obelisks that had survived together since antiquity. As one British historian lamented, '[Luxor's] imposing pylon gate will always have the bereft appearance of an elephant with one tusk missing.'

Not much is certain about the obelisks, but this much seems clear: after carving them out of the quarry, the Egyptians dragged them to the Nile and floated them to their temples. Luckily for them, the Nile runs north, so they could simply hop on this great natural conveyor belt. In fact, the hieroglyph for travelling north was a boat with no mast, and that for heading south was a boat with sail. But what sort of ancient boat could handle a 400-ton payload?

The NOVA team has shown how the Egyptians might have dragged their obelisks to the river. Now they want to gain some insight into what sort of gargantuan boats might have been capable of carrying such monoliths forty centuries ago.

That the ancient Egyptians were expert boatmen is hardly surprising. The Nile was the main life support for their civilization, the spinal cord of an empire. All the major towns and cities were built along it. Pharaohs were often buried with their boats.

'Why did the king need a boat in the afterlife?' Lehner muses. 'Because everybody needed a boat in this life. People great and small, fishermen, noblemen, all had their boats. As a matter of fact, one of the principal inscriptions in people's tombs to show that they were righteous people is that they gave food to the hungry, they gave milk to the thirsty, and they gave boats to the boatless.'

In 1954 Egyptologist Kamal el Mallakh was excavating beneath a wall near the Great Pyramid. He had a hunch that there was a boat pit there: a long narrow hole in the ground where a boat had been buried with a pharaoh in order to provide him transport to the underworld. Such holes had already been discovered on the other side of the pyramid.

Mallakh's hunch paid off: he found a row of limestone blocks, one of them bearing the cartouche of Djedefre, a son of Khufu, the pharaoh who built the Great Pyramid in the twenty-sixth century BC. After petitioning for months for permission to excavate, Mallakh finally began to dig between the blocks, working his way into a vast subterranean cavity. 'When I opened that hole,' he said later, 'I could smell history.'

More specifically, he could smell wood. He had discovered the Solar Bark of Khufu, the oldest boat on

The reconstructed Solar Bark of Khufu, the oldest boat in the world.

earth. A hundred and forty-four feet long, weighing 150 tons, it was buried in 1224 intricate pieces but now sits, reconstructed, in its own museum near the original site. No one knows whether the ship was built to be used for the pharaoh's

A felucca, the classic Egyptian boat, sailing on the Nile near Aswan.

funeral, or simply to be buried with him. Zahi Hawass, the Director General for Giza and Saqqara for Egypt's Supreme Council of Antiquities, believes it served only a symbolic purpose.

The Solar Bark couldn't have carried an obelisk – it was never meant to. Yet it is a stunning example of the remarkable boatmanship of the ancient Egyptians. Owain Roberts, NOVA's boat expert, has come to the museum to learn from Khufu's boat builders. He hopes to build a boat similar to the kind Egyptians might have used to transport obelisks over water.

Roberts, a nautical engineer and historian at the University of Wales, Bangor, regularly works on the reconstruction of historical vessels. A portly fellow of late middle age, in a floppy hat and glasses, he speaks with the easy pace and gentrified accent of a country gentleman. 'They knew all the tricks,' he says as he admires the Solar Bark in the museum. 'They knew about stability of a boat. They knew about locking the timbers together to reduce movement, because movement destroys a boat.

All that restricted them was the fact that they had only wood and rope to do it with.'

But just what kinds of boat did they use to transport obelisks? Again, the only clues come from tombs and temples. Aneni, a high official under Tuthmosis I who oversaw the erection of two obelisks at Karnak, claimed in his tomb that he 'built the "august" boat of 120 cubits [207 feet] in length and 40 cubits [69 feet] in breadth for transporting these obelisks'. Another, more famous rendition of an obelisk-carrying boat is from the mortuary temple of the great female pharaoh, Hatshepsut.

Hatshepsut was originally queen for nine years, while her husband (and half-brother) Tuthmosis II was pharaoh. When he died, his son Tuthmosis III, though still a boy, naturally took over. Hatshepsut at first served as regent to her stepson (whose mother was another, minor wife of Tuthmosis II). Before long, however, she declared herself pharaoh and demoted Tuthmosis III to co-regent. She insisted on being referred to with the masculine pronoun and had herself portrayed in drawings with the traditional artificial beard.

Hatshepsut was a clever politician. Knowing that the people (and, more importantly, the priesthood) might not accept a female pharaoh, particularly when the rightful king was alive and well, she went on a building spree to proclaim her glory. Temples sprouted up all over Egypt and Nubia, honouring various deities and testifying to the greatness of the new pharaoh. Hatshepsut also erected at least four obelisks, two pairs located near her enormous sanctuary at Karnak.

Hatshepsut's inscriptions provide clues to the creation of obelisks that complement the physical evidence provided by the Unfinished Obelisk of Aswan. At the base of her one surviving obelisk are the words:

> *I was sitting in the palace and I remembered the One who created*
> *me; my heart directed me to make for him two obelisks of electrum,*
> *that their pyramidions might mingle with the sky… They are [each]*
> *of one block of enduring granite without joint or flaw therein. My*
> *Majesty began work on them in Year 15, second month of Winter,*
> *day 1, continuing until Year 16, fourth month of Summer, day 30,*
> *making 7 months in cutting from the mountain. I acted for him*
> *with a straightforward heart, as a king does for any god . . . Amun,*
> *Lord of the Thrones of the Two Lands . . . I am his daughter in very*
> *truth, who glorifies him.*

Hatshepsut also provides the most tantalizing clue regarding obelisks' river journeys. In her funerary temple at Deir el-Bahari, west of Thebes, a series of reliefs shows the transport of two of her obelisks from Elephantine to Thebes. A barge carries both obelisks, arranged end to end. Scholars estimate that the barge must have been at least 200 feet long. Twenty-seven boats, arranged in three rows, tow the barge down the Nile.

From these reliefs, experts have concluded that the boat had three separate sets of crossbeams for added strength. It also appears to have had several hogging trusses – structures of rope and wood arching over the deck to keep the bow and stern from collapsing under the weight of the obelisks.

Owain Roberts designed his boat with all this in mind. However, he took some liberties in interpreting the scene. Many experts believe that Hatshepsut's drawing of her boat is, as Reginald Engelbach said, 'an impressionist view'. That is, they feel that the reliefs show two obelisks end to end simply to signify that two obelisks were on one boat. Roberts goes even further, maintaining that the scene merely indicates that two obelisks were transported by boat. This view causes some friction with Lehner, who wonders why Hatshepsut's artists wouldn't draw two boats if two were used, or two obelisks side by side if that's how it was done. 'What you see in Hatshepsut's relief,' he insists, 'is what they used.'

Roberts believes that the soundest type of boat to carry such a load so high out of the water would be a catamaran, which has two separate hulls. He feels that the Hatshepsut relief confirms this: 'You can see there are two overlapping sets of helmsmen, and they're both facing one way, which to my mind tells me straight off there are two boats here.' He is right that the Egyptians, who could draw only in two dimensions, would show multiple objects or people by overlapping their profiles slightly.

'But with the towing boats,' Lehner argues, 'they're showing multiple boats, and you see one and another one and another one, but on the obelisk you just see one prow and one stern.'

The drawing is inconclusive – the front of the boat, where a double-hulled boat might show overlapping outlines, has eroded away – but the best one can say on behalf of Roberts's catamaran theory is that the relief doesn't definitely disprove it. The simpler solution remains a single-hulled boat, and ultimately Roberts agrees to design such a vessel.

When he presents his design to Lehner, the archaeologist is a bit taken aback: 'Whoa, that is wide! A real wide-bodied barge.'

Indeed, Roberts's boat is only twice as long as it is wide. 'In order to carry the weight,' he explains, 'and to have it as high as in Hatshepsut, of course, we had to go for a great beam.' To test his barge, Roberts is charged with the task of loading NOVA's smaller, 2-ton obelisk on to it and taking the boat for a spin down the Nile.

On 19 March 1999 Roberts makes his attempt to shove off from Aswan and float down the Nile, barge, obelisk and all. When his team arrives at the dock on the west bank of the Nile, Roberts's barge is moored and ready to go, its yellow plywood hull rocking placidly on the water. A ramp of mortared stones slopes from the ground up to the deck, with a wooden track sunk into its surface. The 2-ton obelisk, tied to a wooden sledge, rests at the foot of the ramp.

Roberts's son, Iolo, a mechanical engineer and expert rock climber, is the NOVA team's rope man. Father and son use an elaborate system of ropes to lash the obelisk to the sledge and pulley it up the ramp. The obelisk is tied to two main ropes that run around wooden blocks at the end of the ramp and lead back to the dock. Ten men standing on either side of the dock pull on the ropes. The wooden

blocks at the end reverse the direction of force so that the obelisk moves forward.

After shouts of 'Hela hop!' and adjustments by the Robertses, the sledge glides smoothly up the ramp and rests comfortably aboard the ship. The crew and onlookers break into cheers.

A short time later, Roberts stands on his barge as workers push it, gondola-style, out into the open water. A powerboat picks up a tow line, and the barge begins to float down the Nile, as if to be delivered up to Thebes. Watching Roberts's outline in the afternoon sun, one can almost imagine the river journey of Hatshepsut's obelisk, with twenty-seven tugboats, a pilot ship, three boats of high priests, and crowds of onlookers gathering along the shore to catch a glimpse of the pharaoh's glory floating down the river.

After travelling downstream for several days, a great obelisk-barge en route from the quarry would approach the southern outskirts of the city of Thebes. Merely a district capital during the Old Kingdom, Thebes became the national capital when Ahmose (1570–1546 BC) overthrew the invading Hyskos and founded the Eighteenth Dynasty – the first of the New Kingdom. For the next 500 years, Thebes was the centre of the civilized world. As the pharaohs conquered distant lands, riches poured into their capital and monuments sprang up commemorating the great kings. Homer wrote in the *Iliad* that 'in Egyptian Thebes the heaps of precious ingots gleam… [and] twice ten score in martial state of valiant men with steeds and chariots march through each massy gate'. Those sailing with the obelisk could gaze at the avenue of sphinxes, the royal palaces, and the villas and lesser buildings of the great city.

The obelisk would sail right by the city and pull into dock a little way north, on the eastern shore. Across the water to the west, lining two miles of the desert's periphery, was a row of funerary temples. Beyond them, hundreds of tombs had been cut into the cliffs and valleys – the City of the Dead. On the north and south sides, respectively, were the Valley of the Kings and the Valley of the Queens. In the tombs between lay the viziers, stewards, generals, sculptors, treasurers, priests and other deceased nobles who served their sovereigns. Despite its name, the City of the Dead was bustling with studios and workshops, houses for the artisans, and even palaces for the kings, from which they might survey the work that would pave their way to the afterlife.

The obelisk, however, was destined for the east side of the river, inside the 150-acre agglomeration of temples and shrines, pylons and colonnades, statues and obelisks that was Karnak. Upon docking, the obelisk party would be greeted by soldiers running down from the temples holding branches aloft. The inhabitants of Thebes would flock to the shore to watch the ceremonies; it would be akin to a national holiday. Priests would make sacrifices and present offerings to the gods. The crew would then use another ramp to slide the obelisk on its sledge to its appointed place in the park of treasures.

No matter which pharaoh had commissioned this obelisk, his steward would face the same daunting task: to raise it to a vertical position atop a pedestal. If he succeeded, he would be rewarded with great riches. In what is probably an apocryphal story, Pliny the Elder wrote that Rameses the Great had his own son tied to the tip of an obelisk to ensure that his workers would take extra care. (Since he had hundreds of sons, he probably considered the ploy merely an amusing added incentive; certainly the workers knew what fate awaited them if they failed.)

Though the ancient Egyptians were meticulous in recording when and where they erected their obelisks, they didn't think to mention how. Like others who have sought to raise obelisks before him, Mark Whitby has had to devise methods of his own that the ancients could have used.

Rather than try to float the 25-ton obelisk 150 miles down river to Karnak, Whitby will try to raise the 25-tonner back at Rashwan's quarry in Aswan. The gods may be displeased: on the day his team is to begin, the *khamasin* strikes. *Khamasin* means 'fifty' in Arabic; it is the dry, hot wind that storms in from the desert and can last as long as fifty days. It turns Aswan into a dust bowl and sweeps away any idea of beginning work. As it happens, the wind dies down the following day. But in the interlude, the NOVA team's thoughts turn to the successes – and failures – of their past attempts.

In the 1995 attempt, sculptor Martin Isler raised a small 2-ton obelisk using a system similar to that which was successful in NOVA's 1998 Easter Island project. Lifting the obelisk with levers and placing small stones under it as they went along, his team raised it to an angle of 40 degrees. It was then easy to pull the obelisk the rest of the way up with ropes. But when it came to the larger, 40-ton model, levers alone would not have done the trick.

The team was led by Ali el Gasab, a tall, slender, flamboyant man whose expertise lay in transporting antiquities for the Egyptian government. He designed a system that involved mounting the sledge on rollers and pushing it over a shallow ramp that led down to a pedestal. The crew had no problem getting the sledge over the edge; then they used ropes attached to its top to control its descent down the ramp. Slowly they lowered the sledge until the bottom edge of the obelisk settled perfectly into a turning groove in the pedestal. (Ancient pedestals had a straight groove chiselled on to their tops, into which an obelisk could be placed and then tipped upright. Without such a notch, it would have been virtually impossible to raise an obelisk into exactly the right position to face the rising sun. Turning it once it was upright would have been too difficult.)

When their obelisk settled into its turning groove, Ali's Egyptian workers let out a whoop and lifted him into the air in celebration. Indeed, it was quite a feat to have placed this colossal stone perfectly into place. With the obelisk at a 32-degree angle, the rest seemed easy. The plan was to use levers to increase the angle and then, just as with the smaller model, have teams of men simply pull the obelisk up the rest of the way with ropes.

The heavier weight, though, changed the ball game. The workers quickly reached an angle of 40 degrees, but after that they could no longer get the leverage they needed. Two hundred men tugged at ropes on the other side of the pedestal, but they succeeded only in forcing the bottom edge deeper into the turning groove.

With one day left, Roger Hopkins threw together a wooden A-frame and lashed the ropes to the top of it, raising the angle to increase their pulling force. But now not enough workers could reach the rope – the portion near the A-frame was too high off the ground. After pulling all day, the team had added only two degrees to the angle of incline. The obelisk was stuck at 42 degrees.

A different angle ramp, a better-designed A-frame, longer ropes: any or all of these might have made Ali's method pay off. But, a week behind schedule and further over budget every hour, the team had to accept defeat.

The 40-ton obelisk lies on the ramp, its base in the turning groove, as pulling crews struggle in vain to haul it upright.

Four years later, Lehner and Hopkins are back, along with Whitby. They have had plenty of time to mull over the frustrations of the first attempt in the hope of devising a successful strategy.

Lehner muses on the lessons of defeat. 'Well, I'm no engineer, but it's my impression that the reason we didn't get the obelisk up last time is because the ramp wasn't high enough, the slope down to the pedestal wasn't steep enough, and the pulling ramp on the other side of the pedestal was not high enough. For a while, I thought that if all these things were corrected, Ali Gasab would have gotten it up. But then I started to wonder if some vital ingredient wasn't missing. The more I thought about it, it seemed to me we were just not doing something right. I thought it was worth another look at all the evidence, all of Egyptian technology.'

Studying the ancient technology put certain limits on the NOVA team's planning. For one thing, pulleys – which might seem an obvious solution to the problem at hand – were not an option. Pulleys were probably invented some time during the Middle Kingdom, several hundred years before the New Kingdom, but they would have had to be constructed of wood. There was no iron or steel available in ancient Egypt, and a wooden pulley would not have been strong enough to lift an obelisk. Levers, too, were probably not the solution. They worked well with the 2-ton obelisk, but even the 40-ton stone exposed the limitations of levers. It was simply too difficult to gain leverage after reaching an angle of 40 degrees. 'It would have been exponentially more problematic for a 450-ton obelisk,' notes Lehner.

An ancient turning groove from the temple at Luxor.

Something different was needed, and Mark Whitby was drafted to mastermind the new approach. In his mind, improving the A-frame or having men pull from higher ground behind the pedestal was the wrong approach. 'Our goal,' he says now, 'is to get the obelisk to as steep an angle as possible' before it settles into the turning groove. Then it will be a relatively easy job to gently pull it to a vertical position. Whitby set his sights high: 'We're thinking of about 75 to 80 degrees,' he says. 'And from that point onwards, it's a case of just easing it over.'

It would be too dangerous, however, to use a ramp at such a steep angle. Instead, Whitby has designed a wooden framework for the obelisk which can be tipped over a wall and eased right down on to the pedestal.

'You've got to try to get the stone to do as much of the work as possible,' he explains. 'But you've also got to be in control all the time. And that's the art.'

One of the keys to Whitby's plan is manipulating the obelisk's centre of gravity. The centre of gravity on a pencil is the point at which you can balance it on your finger. If you push a pencil, or an obelisk, over the edge of a table or cliff, it will begin to tip over when its centre of gravity reaches the edge. Whitby designed his wooden frame so that its pivot point, which will be at the edge of the ramp while the obelisk is being tipped downward, will be about 5 feet below the centre of gravity. This means that more force will be needed to tip the obelisk, but it also means that workers can tip it with more control.

Whitby uses a miniature model of the frame and obelisk to demonstrate his system to the NOVA team. 'By reducing the height of the ramp, placing the turning point in front of the centre of gravity, and applying a force on the butt end instead of the tip end, we're going to keep it in control.' He plans to use a 'swigging' process to tip the obelisk. A granite block will serve as a counterweight, tied to the bottom of the obelisk with two sets of vertical ropes and set on the ground next to the pedestal. Horizontal ropes will be tied to one pair of vertical ropes, and workers will pull on the horizontal ropes to tug the obelisk downward. (To see how this works, stretch a rubber band around your left thumb and forefinger. Then insert your right thumb and forefinger into the rubber band and spread them apart. You can feel the tension increasing on your left finger and thumb as the rubber band spreads sideways.)

Each tug on the ropes should tip the obelisk about five degrees. As it begins to tip upward, workers on the ramp will prop up the obelisk with wooden blocks, while those below will tighten the second set of vertical butt-end ropes for the next tug. Then the pullers can release the swigging ropes and rest before the next tug.

When the obelisk reaches an angle of 61 degrees, the centre of gravity will lie directly above the pivot point. Theoretically, at this moment the entire contraption could balance perfectly on the edge. But once it tips higher, it will succumb to gravity and slide down on to the pedestal. In order to prevent the obelisk from tumbling uncontrollably, workers positioned at the nose of the obelisk will slow its descent by pulling on two guide ropes secured by logs and boulders. If all goes as planned, the obelisk will approach the pedestal gradually, settling into its turning groove at 81 degrees. At that point it should be easy to pull it to 90 degrees with ropes.

Whitby demonstrates the process flawlessly with his model. He can't help but be optimistic. 'This mechanism is a bit of an ingenious device,' he says with a smirk, 'and that's exactly what engineer means – an ingenious person.'

All during the carving, sliding and boat experiments, Rick Brown and his son Wyly have been hard at work building Whitby's wooden frame, which they call 'the Hand of God' partly because it resembles a handful of spread fingers. They are members of the Timber Framers' Guild, the same group that build the NOVA trebuchets at Loch Ness (Chapter 1). All week long, they have laboured in a special workshop they set up near the pedestal. Because they were forced to use existing pieces of yellow pine that were much larger than they needed, the framework turned out larger and bulkier than designed, but there is no reason to believe this would compromise the chances of success.

Using 'swigging' to raise an obelisk

1. Obelisk at rest

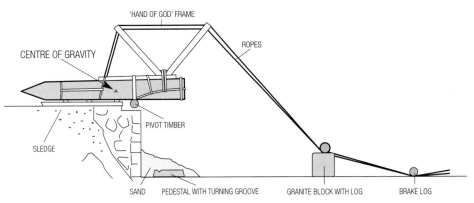

'HAND OF GOD' FRAME

CENTRE OF GRAVITY

ROPES

PIVOT TIMBER

SLEDGE

SAND   PEDESTAL WITH TURNING GROOVE   GRANITE BLOCK WITH LOG   BRAKE LOG

2. Pulling on swigging ropes

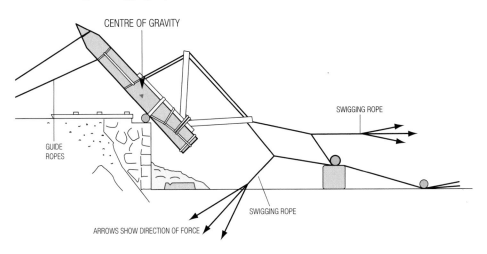

CENTRE OF GRAVITY

SWIGGING ROPE

GUIDE ROPES

SWIGGING ROPE

ARROWS SHOW DIRECTION OF FORCE

Rick Brown takes a break from his final preparations to survey his handiwork. 'You know,' he says, 'the Hand would be worthless without Iolo's lashing.' Iolo and Owain Roberts are overseeing the extravagant system of ropes needed to secure and work the wooden rigging. While the Browns build their frame, the Robertses prepare lengths of thick rope to bind it together and to provide the swigging.

According to Owain Roberts, the Egyptians' seafaring expertise would have come in quite handy when building their obelisk-raising rig. 'They certainly understood the problems of sailing,' he says while tying one of the hundreds of knots he will tie that week. 'You can't manage a boat without rope, and with the cumbersome square rig they were using, miles of rope would have been used. Rope must have been a major business.'

The Hand of God is ready at last. On the morning of 21 March, the obelisk lies naked on its earthen ramp, its pyramidion like a sharpened pencil point. In the early afternoon, the Browns and their Egyptian workers descend on it like a throng of surgeons, placing the wooden framework in place and lashing the parts together precisely. Wyly Brown calls his group 'the Happy Gang'. The Browns and the Egyptian foreman, Abd el-Aleem, join forces enthusiastically even though they aren't able to understand a word of each other's language. 'The trick,' says Wyly, 'is to keep everything in control without offending Abd el-Aleem!'

They manage to assemble the wooden frame around the obelisk just as planned. The Hand begins to form on the bottom half of the obelisk like a huge inverted sawhorse, legs splayed in the air. Would the ancient Egyptians really have used such a complex structure to raise their obelisks?

'I wouldn't be surprised if this thing works,' says Lehner, 'but what evidence is there that this contraption existed in ancient Egypt?'

'We know they were nautical people,' Whitby responds. 'They built boats to transport 800 tons.'

'Owain,' Lehner turns to his nautical expert, 'is there anything on a boat in ancient Egypt that looks like that?'

'Well,' comes the steady reply, 'the nearest thing is an A-frame. I'm not uncomfortable with that structure, though. To build a cradle for an obelisk, you'd *have* to go into a massive structure.'

Lehner is unconvinced. 'I don't see any evidence in Egyptian boat scenes or tomb scenes of this kind of complexity of rig. I'm sure it will work, but there's no evidence that shows this is probable. The picture we have from the evidence is of organizing people, not making a failsafe, complex system. It's people, ramps and levers.'

A little later, Whitby and his colleague, Henry Woodlock, sit in the shade of the prone obelisk, in turban and cricket cap respectively, going over every aspect of the raising. Lehner may think their method too modern, too engineered, but they at least want to ensure that it will work. Then others can debate how authentic it was. They scribble in notebooks, going over their calculations, making sure that the obelisk will come down neatly into the turning groove. In particular, Whitby is concerned about the possibility that the ropes will stretch.

Roger Hopkins has already voiced his concern on that front. 'Lots of bells and whistles here,' he said earlier. 'Wood joining with other pieces of wood, lot of ropes: all negatives in my book.'

Roberts, on the other hand, has insisted there's no problem: 'You want more strength, you just put in more ropes.'

Going over the final details with Woodlock, Whitby seems optimistic. 'I think we've got quite a bit covered,' he says.

The next day, the Browns finish lashing the frame to the butt end of the obelisk. Then they and their gang move the obelisk forward, positioning it as planned with the centre of gravity about 5 feet shy of the edge of the ramp and the giant pivot timber. Working with Iolo Roberts, they lash the pivot timber to the obelisk.

Sandpit method. Side view

1. Obelisk is levered to edge of ramp.

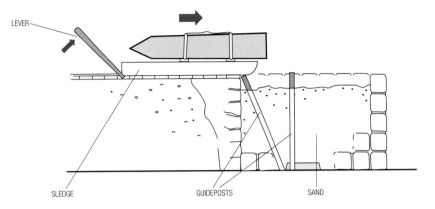

LEVER

SLEDGE   GUIDEPOSTS   SAND

2. Sand is removed by hand.

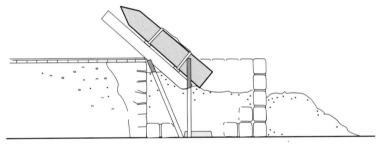

GUIDEPOSTS INDICATE LOCATION OF TURNING GROOVE AND PROPER ANGLE FOR OBELISK'S DESCENT.

3. Obelisk rests in turning groove.

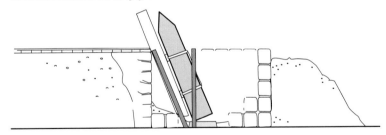

4. Obelisk is pulled to vertical.

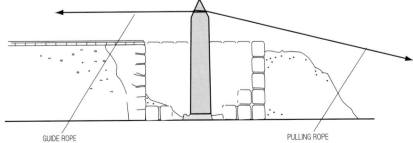

GUIDE ROPE   PULLING ROPE

Everything is in order. The obelisk lies on its ramp just as in all the drawings, the great inverted sawhorse on top, the entire contraption just waiting to be pulled into life. Its bottom end hangs over the abyss. Below is the pedestal, covered with a pile of sand to cushion the obelisk and help the men guide it into the turning groove. Next to the pedestal is the counterweight, tied to the frame with vertical ropes. The whole thing is a marvellous manifestation of carefully drawn plans – Frankenstein's monster awaiting its jolt of electricity.

In the meantime, Roger Hopkins has been pursuing a five-year-old obsession. During NOVA's 1995 experiments, he had erected a 2-ton obelisk using the 'sandpit' method, and in 1999 he hopes to improve on his success. He remains convinced that this is how the Egyptians put up their 400-ton stones.

In all the thousands of ancient Egyptian texts uncovered by archaeologists, there is but one that contains any clue as to how large monuments were erected. Known as the Papyrus Anastasi, it dates from the time of Rameses II and measures 8 inches high and 27 feet long. In it, one scribe writes to another, poking fun at him for having failed in his commissions and declaring that he will now outdo his rival at all such tasks. He writes mockingly: 'Come, good sir, vigilant scribe, who art at the head of the army…! A despatch has come from the crown-prince… telling that an obelisk has been newly made, graven with the name of His Majesty, of 110 cubits in length of shaft; its pedestal 10 cubits [square], the block at its base making 7 cubits in every direction… its pyramidion one cubit in height, its point measuring two fingers. Add them together… so that thou mayest appoint every man needed to drag them and send them to the Red Mountain [the Gebel Ahmar quarry]… Answer quickly, do not dawdle!' To grasp the scale of the obelisk described, it's helpful to know that a cubit equals 20 inches.

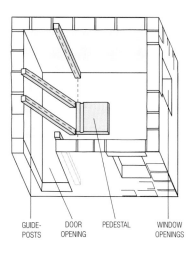

Sandpit method. Top view

GUIDE-POSTS   DOOR OPENING   PEDESTAL   WINDOW OPENINGS

The author later challenges his friend to direct the erection of a colossal monument, possibly a statue: 'It is said to thee: Empty the magazine that has been loaded with sand under the monument of thy Lord which had been brought from the Red Mountain. It makes 30 cubits stretched upon the ground, and 20 cubits in breadth, _____ed with 100[?] chambers filled with sand from the river-bank… How many men will [it take to] demolish it in six hours… so that the monument may be established in its place? It is Pharaoh's desire to see it beautiful!' It is unclear whether the measurements here refer to the monument or to the magazine, or sand pit, under the monument.

Based on this text, Reginald Engelbach proposed a method by which an obelisk would be let down into a funnel-shaped, sand-filled pit. The pit would be built of mud bricks – the most common building material in both ancient and modern Egypt. Once the obelisk was tipped over the edge of the pit and rested on the pile of sand, the sand would be scooped out in baskets removed through tunnels. As the sand was removed, the obelisk's own weight would lower it deeper and deeper into the pit. Eventually it would be guided on to its turning groove and then pulled to a vertical position.

In 1995 Hopkins actually used a form of this method to put up the 2-ton obelisk. Both Martin Isler and Mark Lehner were sceptical, wondering how Hopkins could possibly ensure that the obelisk would hit its turning groove. But Hopkins insisted that if the sand was removed slowly and carefully, workers could make adjustments as they went. Rashwan was fearful for the safety of his workers, and indeed some of the adjustments had to be made by someone crawling into the pit and risking life and limb to shovel a bit of sand out of the way. But sure enough, when all the sand had finally flowed out of the pit, Hopkins's obelisk had found its mark. After that, it was easy to pull the obelisk upright with ropes.

His colleagues put it down to beginner's luck, but Hopkins was convinced that this was how the ancients had erected their colossal obelisks. In 1999, he begged for the chance to try it on the 25-ton stone, but again he was given only the 2-tonner.

This time, Hopkins has refined his sandpit to ensure extra accuracy. The mud-brick wall has two doors at the bottom which he can open separately to let sand run out of either side as needed. The key modification is the addition of wooden posts – guide rails that Hopkins will use to estimate the correct angle of the obelisk as it descends in order to lead the base directly to the turning groove.

On 23 March, all systems are go for the sandpit. Using a crane to save time, Hopkins has his obelisk lifted on to a trackway. With the help of several workers, he levers it butt-first along the track and over the edge, so that its bottom rests on the top of the pile of sand. Then he and his helpers step inside the pit and begin to shovel sand out of the doors at the bottom. As the sand sinks lower, they use their hands to scoop it out, reaching directly under the butt of the tilted obelisk. Suddenly the obelisk shifts, settling lower in the pit. Onlookers gasp. Hopkins straightens up and calls out: 'What's the worst that can happen, I lose a hand, an arm? No problem.'

The obelisk slides deeper, inching along its guide rails. Whitby, watching, remains unimpressed: 'When you're moving these heavy stones around, you've got to have absolute control over them. Imagine this for real with a 300-ton obelisk.'

'Actually,' Hopkins answers, 'I see a definite advantage to a heavier obelisk with this method. This one is so light compared to the sledge that the sledge is hanging up the free fall.'

In the years since the first attempt, Lehner has come around to Hopkins's method. 'At first, I didn't like the sand method,' he says, 'but in the last few years, I've looked at ancient Egyptian evidence like the Papyrus Anastasi, and I've considered the advantages Roger has pointed out. And now, as an Egyptologist, I would have to say that sand is the most probable method.'

Soon he and Hopkins are both in the pit, scooping the last bits of sand away, and at last the obelisk slides compliantly into the turning groove. 'Looks like you hit it spot on,' says Lehner.

The obelisk leans at a 60-degree angle. Early the next morning, Hopkins's team pulls it upright within minutes, as his eight pullers chant 'Rah-ger,' cheering when it finally reaches 90 degrees. Whitby points out that a 60-degree angle would not be steep enough to pull a full-scale obelisk upright. His method is designed to land the obelisk at 80 degrees, in order to ease the burden on the pullers. Still, Hopkins has erected two obelisks now, which is two more than anyone present.

The main advantages of the sand method, according to Hopkins, are simplicity and safety. 'I have a lot of respect for engineers,' he says, 'but we always learned as children to appreciate common sense, and everything we've done here has been an extension of common sense. The obelisk was a very fragile and precious piece of stone, and it had to be treated as such. It couldn't be whipped around and left dangling.'

At 3.30 the previous afternoon, in another part of the quarry, Iolo Roberts's crew has finished tying Spanish windlasses and other fancy knots to attach the vertical ropes running from the large obelisk to the counterweight and the two swigging ropes leading horizontally off the vertical ropes. The entire Whitby apparatus is now ready. While an Egyptian worker leisurely sweeps the area around the obelisk,

Workers lever Hopkins' small obelisk along the ramp to the sandpit.

the raising crew holds a briefing to agree on simple hand signals to signify 'pull'. 'walk', 'hold' and 'release' — and, in case of an emergency, 'run!' It's no joke: no one knows how the 25-ton obelisk will behave in the Hand of God.

Wyly Brown calls for a moment of silence, and then the forty labourers from Aswan split into two groups, twenty men on each swigging rope. An additional three men stand off to each side of the obelisk, holding ropes lashed to the pyramidion, to keep the obelisk aligned on the horizontal axis. Whitby chants the first 'Hela hop!' and the forty men lean back on their ropes. The Browns and Robertses flinch as the yellow pine beams groan, but the obelisk rises ever so slightly off its rollers. Henry Woodlock and Rick Brown quickly slide wooden blocks under it to prop it up, Iolo Roberts and Wyle Brown rush in to tighten the holding ropes, and Whitby signals the pullers to release. Then they tighten the swigging ropes as well.

Opposite The small obelisk stands at 90 degrees in the emptied sandpit.

Left Using the Hand of God rigging devised by the Browns, the pulling team attempts to pull the 25-ton obelisk upright.

So far, so good. If this keeps up, the pivot log will make contact with the platform and then roll to the edge, keeping its position relative to the obelisk. 'I think maybe it'll be two or three pulls before it actually comes down onto this bearing,' says Whitby. 'So I think we're doing quite well. It's not a bad system.' He speaks a little too soon, though, for when the pivot log does make contact, it has shifted in relation to the obelisk and is now too close to the edge.

After workers knock the log back into place, the team repeats the swigging process six or eight times. By five in the afternoon, the obelisk has risen from the horizontal only about 10 degrees and Whitby calls a halt to the day's work. They will try to finish off the job the next day – the final day of filming.

As the crew members pick up their belongings and disperse for the night, the obelisk sits moored by her ropes and timbers, tilted slightly upwards, pointing directly at the setting sun. Amun must be pleased.

Why 'swigging' failed

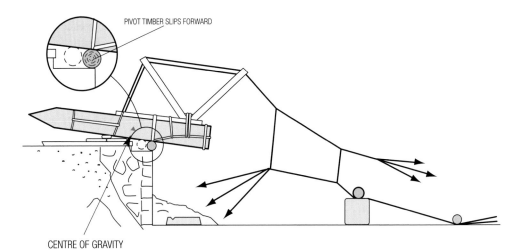

PIVOT TIMBER SLIPS FORWARD

CENTRE OF GRAVITY

Some hundred years after Hatshepsut and her stepson Tuthmosis III erected their great obelisks at Karnak and Luxor, the cult of Amun-Ra and obelisks fell out of favour. The pharaoh Amenophis IV (*circa* 1400 BC), whose name meant 'Amun is satisfied', changed his name to Akhenaten, 'Beneficial to Aten', a new god symbolized by the sun disc. Just as the Rapanui who overthrew the *moai* cult overturned all its statues, so Akhenaten ordered all references to Amun obliterated, including hieroglyphics carved high on existing obelisks. Only one obelisk is known to date from Akhenaten's reign, and none has been found from the reigns of his three successors. Few if any obelisks appear to have built for several hundred years, as the Egyptian empire went through a period of upheaval and relative weakness. There was a resurgence under the reign of Rameses II, the greatest monument-builder of them all, but after him another fallow period ensued, during which Egypt was divided into smaller states, often ruled by foreign kings. Although native pharaohs did make a comeback in the seventh and sixth centuries BC, the Egyptian empire was in decline. Persia ruled the area ruthlessly until Alexander the Great invaded in 332 BC and Greek rule of Egypt began. The age of obelisks was over.

Three thousand years after Rameses II, Mark Whitby is given one last day to try to raise his obelisk. The morning does not begin well. Whitby has ordered the timbers beneath the counterweight removed, so the weight will hang free, exerting extra force on the butt end of the obelisk. This will make it easier for the pullers to tilt the obelisk. Yesterday the pivot log was not yet in contact with the platform, so the obelisk was pivoting on a wooden chock set just below its centre of gravity. But now that the pivot log has made contact with the platform, the obelisk must pivot on the log, which is set at a point several feet to the right of its centre of gravity.

This makes the pullers' task much harder.

When the timbers are removed, however, the ropes stretch and the great granite block just sinks to the ground. And when the swigging operation begins again, Whitby discovers that without the counterweight the pullers can't generate enough force to tilt the obelisk.

Iolo Roberts and Wyly Brown work feverishly to tighten all the ropes, and workmen try to lever the counterweight back on to the stack of timber. But it's taking too long. Finally Whitby orders the crane brought in to do the job. With everything in place, Whitby's ineluctable confidence seeps back into his voice: 'I think this next go will do it.' It is 10 am, and he has a flight to catch at six in the evening.

Soon his confidence is deflated, however. At 10.30, the timber stack is pulled out from under the counterweight and the obelisk begins to tip. But once again, the ropes stretch and the weight sinks to the ground. 'The bloody rope slipped!' he cries. An hour later, the rope holding the weight breaks completely. An hour after that, with everything retied, two more main ropes snap, sending the crane that had been holding the weight reeling back violently. Iolo Roberts, the rope man, throws his hat down in frustration. At an impasse, the group decides to break for lunch.

Near the end of the break, Whitby can't help commenting that the problem with the system lies with the rope knots. 'These ropes just aren't making it, Iolo. We've got to make a knot that works, or we've got to find another way of doing it.' Roberts storms off in a rage.

Surveying the state of the project after lunch, Whitby sighs. 'Personally, I now feel like the sandpit method might have been the best way of doing the job.' But he won't give up on his rig yet. Whitby finally decides to abandon the counterweight and go with manpower, like the ancients. He orders extra men brought in, and by 2.30 120 pullers are assembled. At four o'clock the swiggers, divided among six ropes, hela hop. The obelisk begins to rise but, as it rises, it rocks dangerously from side to side, forcing the pivot timber towards the edge of the ramp. Whitby calls a halt.

'Is there a danger the pivot timber will fall off the end?' Lehner asks him.

'It's not a danger,' Whitby groans, 'it's a reality.' Crew members work for half an hour to get the pivot timber back in place, but when the swiggers pull again, the pivot continues to roll out of position.

'All the work that's gone into this,' pants Roberts, 'and it might just defeat us.'

'Bring in the crane!' Whitby cries, as the sun descends ever closer to the horizon. The monstrous machine, left over from the building of the Aswan High Dam, roars and crawls into position, lifting the obelisk while workers scurry underneath to reposition the timber. By the time the obelisk has been set back down – now back in a horizontal position – it is too late to begin swigging again. Whitby decides to miss his flight, and the team agrees to extend the project one more day. Late that night, however, Whitby and the others agree that the setup is simply too dangerous. They announce that they are calling off the attempt.

The next morning, the team wanders around the quarry picking up and sorting out what has happened. They try not to talk about the obvious contrast between Whitby's abandoned rig and Hopkins's 2-ton obelisk standing nearby, erect as a flagpole.

'I've learned that in some respects we've overcomplicated the problem,' Whitby admits. 'If I had to do this again, I'd use a combination of this way and the sandpit way. I'd simplify the framework on the top to just a very large tree trunk, and I'd bring the pivot point back a bit. Then I would land the obelisk in a pile of sand.

'To be beaten by a 25-ton obelisk when ancient people were putting up 400-ton obelisks is a real blow to one's professional pride. The Egyptians did it beautifully with a 400-ton obelisk. If we can't do it with a little one, we really aren't that clever.'

Hopkins, nearby, tries not to gloat. 'I feel we've reached a point that we can conclude that they probably didn't use a fancy, intricate method using levers and

The 25-ton obelisk rests on the ramp, poised at about the highest angle the pulling team was able to achieve.

wood and rope.' As he says, Whitby's method was ingeniously engineered — ' but that's the problem when you try to get too smart with this kind of project.' Lehner agrees. 'When engineers come and try to figure these things out,' he points out, 'it can be extraordinarily insightful. But on the other hand, sometimes engineers tend to get a little too clever. And although they use the tools and techniques that the ancients used, they combine them in various ways that seem counter-intuitive to an Egyptologist. They attribute ways of thinking and ways of calculating to the ancient Egyptians that the Egyptians themselves would not have had. In my mind, the counterweight put it over the edge of complexity.' Hopkins wanders over to his small obelisk and ponders what might have been. 'I would sure love the opportunity to get a big stone like that other one, or even bigger,' he muses, 'and try the sandpit method.'

Hopkins is not alone in his frustration. Flying home over the Atlantic, Rick and Wyly Brown stew over how the obelisk erection, in their opinion, should have been accomplished. The Browns had been brought to Egypt for their skills as timber framers, which they had proved during the trebuchet project in Scotland. When they couldn't help but make suggestions to improve the Hopkins and Whitby apparatuses, it was politely implied that they should go back to their workshop and finish the Hand of God as directed.

Now, instead of sleeping or reading paperbacks, they are hunched over their foldout trays drawing up a list they would call 'The Forty Points of Failure'– forty small ways in which the approach to putting up the obelisk might have been better: simpler, more effective, more authentic. By the time they disembark in Boston, they have already worked out the basics of a system that they feel sure could raise a large obelisk in a historically authentic manner. Like Hopkins, they long to prove the power of sand.

The Browns' proposal, completed soon after their return home, is utterly convincing. Although they are not archaeologists, their commitment to historical authenticity is impressive. They have anticipated every complication, attended to every detail. 'We've looked at the nature of the materials available to the Egyptians,' Rick Brown says. 'And we've looked at the way that early people would have looked at them. They had sand, and they had stone, some wood, and enough natural fibre along the Nile to make ropes with. When you work with these materials, they assume a voice, they speak, and if you listen you can use their power. The Egyptians really understood this, I think. These processes when understood are very simple, elegant, powerful.'

Brown and his son are charged with saving the day – and the challenge of raising another 25-ton obelisk by the end of the summer.

It's as sunny and hot as Egypt, but it's only late August in Massachusetts as the Browns put the finishing touches on their apparatus. The NOVA team has arranged this final attempt closer to home, in the Fletcher Granite quarry in the town of Chelmsford, 25 miles northwest of Boston. Rick and Wyly Brown, along with some colleagues and students from the Timber Framers' Guild and the Massachusetts College of Art, roam around a ramp of 'crush-and-run' gravel which rises to meet a wall of giant granite blocks at its high end. Lying on the ramp is a new 25-ton obelisk, freshly hewn from New Hampshire granite by the Fletcher Granite crew, as smoothly finished as a national monument. Adjoining the ramp is a concrete enclosure filled with sand. Buried somewhere under the sand is the pedestal with its turning groove.

Up to this point, the setup is similar to Hopkins' sandpit in Aswan. But the Browns have added a number of new features to their design. 'Roger was following the basic idea of Engelbach and others,' Rick Brown says, 'but in my opinion trying to slide the obelisk down through the sand just like that is like trying to drive a car without a steering wheel.'

'We're using ropes as steering devices,' he says, and even as he speaks workers are tying a grommet of two-inch-thick Manila rope around the obelisk's pyramidion. A set of three-inch ropes tied to braking timbers will wrap around the butt end, bracing it like a cradle. Additional ropes will be pulled from either side for lateral control.

Rope, of course, was the Achilles' heel of Whitby's attempt, but there are important differences here. For one thing, ropes are not being asked to support great weight; they are only meant to steer. Also, they are not being wrapped around any sharp edges. Most important, they have already been tested, prestretched, and retested.

When everything is finally in place, the team uses a crane to lift the obelisk and position it at an angle, its butt resting on the top of the sand pile, the rest of its weight on a wooden pivot timber on the edge of the ramp. Now it's time to test the sand-and-rope method.

Watching the obelisk as it tilts gradually into the pit is something like watching the hour hand move around the face of a clock. For two days, workers in hard hats and surgical masks, obscured by clouds of dust, shovel and hoe sand out through openings at the bottom of the sandpit. With the sand reaching a temperature of 130 degrees, they get a hint of the experience of being real Egyptian labourers. Every half-hour or so, a sudden creaking of the ropes and the braking timbers announces a shift. The obelisk rotates ever so slightly on the wooden pivot log set at its centre of gravity, and the butt end lowers a few more inches.

'While Roger was using the sand like a sliding board, we're using it like a fluid,' says Brown. 'The obelisk is going to float down into the turning groove, and we're just using the ropes to control it.'

Around noon on the second day, the obelisk passes the critical angle of 45 degrees, after which the obelisk has to be restrained from tipping off the ramp. After lunch, it lurches from 52 degrees to 58 degrees in one heart-stopping little rush of sand. 'It's very fractal,' Mark Lehner says admiringly. 'A little avalanche within a bigger avalanche.' As though in a natural process, the sand flows out the portals in small increments, metamorphosing the sand pile and steadily sharpening the 'angle of repose' of the obelisk.

Most onlookers are impressed at the clocklike precision of the system. Roger Hopkins, though, who has driven up to watch, is doing a self-described 'slow burn' in the background. Although he has been advocating the sandpit method for five years, he had no time in his schedule this year to mount a full-scale obelisk attempt. Now he stands at the side as a critical observer.

'I'm mystified by the need for ropes,' he says. 'They still don't believe me that you can do everything right in the sand. You just have to get right in the pit, as I'm sure the Egyptians were perfectly willing to do. These people are just so petrified of someone getting hurt.'

'Get in there,' he calls out, half-heartedly ribbing them. 'It's too slow. Get in there and pull that sand out of there.' But no one seems to hear.

Late the second afternoon, a cheer erupts from deep in the sandpit. The obelisk has come to rest against the ramp wall at the desired angle of 75 degrees. Only a foot and a half of sand still separates the butt end from the turning groove.

Even this last eighteen inches takes over three hours. First the workers in charge of the braking ropes loosen them a bit. Then the sandmen hoe out some more sand until the obelisk shifts down and engages the ropes again. They repeat the process until, at about 7.30 pm, Wyly Brown's voice wafts up from the pit: 'We're in the turning groove.' There's no celebration yet, however, as workers continue to sweep sand off the pedestal – careful to keep their hands clear – to make certain that the obelisk is resting on stone, not sand.

It is, and at 7.50 pm the celebration begins. 'It came down to within a quarter inch,' Rick Brown says proudly, 'and then it just sat down so gently, never out of control.'

The 25-ton obelisk rests at an angle in the sandpit at the Chelmsford quarry. Workers remove the sand to lower the obelisk into the turning groove.

Right Once the sand has been cleared away and the obelisk rests in the turning groove, the pulling team pulls the obelisk upright.

Opposite The Chelmsford obelisk stands proudly upright at the end of the day, the culmination of a four-year effort.

For ten days the obelisk rests at its 75 degree angle of repose, safely wedged between pedestal and ramp. Wind and rains come and go, sun and moon. 'There was probably a waiting period like this in ancient Egypt,' says Rick Brown one tranquil morning. 'Now they could dismantle the sandpit, as we've done, and clean the pedestal and surrounding area. Then the Pharaoh and his entourage could arrive, and the crowds of course, and have their ceremonies, before the imperial pulling guard finally pulled the thing upright.'

On the appointed day – a sunny, crisp September 10 – the imperial pulling guard at Fletcher Granite consists of 112 art students, timber framers, and assorted volunteers. Twenty-eight-person teams are to pull on four ropes that are braided into one thick cord tied to the obelisk's pyramidion. The braking ropes, tied to the braking timbers, will control the process, along with two other ropes tied to either side. Nothing has been left to chance. The pulling team has even undergone a training session with their leader, Joel McCarty, president of the Timber Framers' Guild and expert in manual barn-raising.

All the numbers have been worked out. The side ropes have 1,000 pounds of tension each, with swigging ropes set up in case more tension is needed. It will take 4,800 pounds of pull to get the obelisk moving, after which the amount of necessary force will diminish rapidly. At 86.5 degrees, the obelisk will become 'self-righting' and begin to tip over on its own accord.

Once the teams are in place and the operation is ready to begin, the rest can only be described as anticlimactic. In less than two minutes, the obelisk rises and settles flat on the pedestal, with hardly a sound. NOVA's quest, consuming five years and three projects, is finally at an end.

The entire crew crowds around the monument, basking in its glory. 'I'm sure this would work on an even larger obelisk,' says Brown. 'We ran the numbers for a hundred-ton, or even five-hundred-ton stone, and I believe we could do it.'

Roger Hopkins, though, is less than ecstatic. 'I'm glad they got it up finally,' he says. 'The fact that it was so uneventful lends a lot of credence to the sandpit method. But I'm disappointed that they had to use such overkill to do it. We could have done it with just sand. They were just unwilling to let there be any chance of something going wrong.'

That was the whole point, according to Brown. 'Given the amount of time and labour and expense they spent making these things, [the Egyptians] would never have settled for vulnerability and loss of control. You think that with Pharaoh's eyes always on them, they wouldn't have micro-managed every detail just as we have?'

Mark Lehner, as pleased as anyone to finally see the obelisk quest accomplished, agrees: the Brown project couldn't have gone better. Surely the ancient Egyptians wanted no risky thrills during the erection of their monuments. 'Sacrificing drama of the moment for control,' he notes, 'gives you a dramatic result which might last thousands of years.'

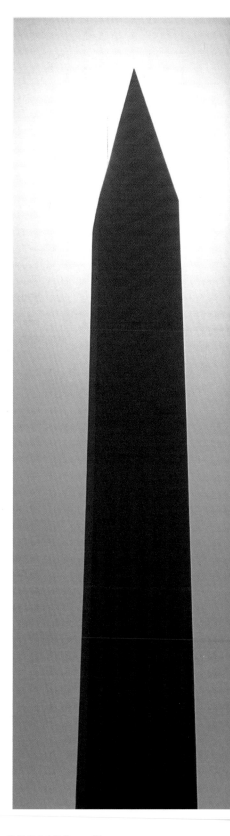

3

EASTER
ISLAND

EASTER SUNDAY, AND A SHIP CRAWLS WESTWARD
ACROSS THOUSANDS OF MILES OF EMPTY PACIFIC
OCEAN. FINALLY, OVER THE HORIZON, A LONE ISLAND
SKIMS INTO VIEW. FOURTEEN HUNDRED MILES FROM
THE NEAREST INHABITED LAND, IT APPEARS BARREN AT
FIRST. RUGGED HILLS, NAKED TO THE WINDS, GIVE
WAY TO GRASSY VOLCANIC CRATERS LITTERED WITH
MILLIONS OF BLACK BASALT ROCKS. SURF POUNDS THE
TWISTING COASTLINE.

Previous page

Majestic and impassive, this moai *carved from volcanic rock stands on the hillside of the quarry where it was abandoned.*

Above

The ahu *at Tahai, located near the harbour of Honga Roa, is believed to be one of the oldest* ahu *structures on the island.*

A s the ship draws closer, however, signs of habitation appear: a few dirt roads criss-crossing the island; a cluster of buildings by the harbour; islanders congregating to welcome the outsiders. And finally, rising from platforms set along the shore, rows of enormous stone statues emerge, gazing mutely inland, as astonishing and incongruous as Doric columns in this place and time.

The year could be 1722… or 1998. In 1722 the ship was that of Admiral Jacob Roggeveen, sent by the Dutch West India Company to find a low, sandy island sighted thirty-five years before. In 1998 the vessel is a commercial airliner flying in from Tahiti, and its passengers include NOVA's team of scientists, who have come in hopes of unravelling some of the mysteries that have surrounded the island since Roggeveen's voyage.

Roggeveen named the place Easter Island, in honour of the date of his arrival. Twenty-three hundred miles from the nearest major population centre, it is the most remote inhabited island on the planet, famous both for the utter isolation of

the civilization it once harboured and for the statues its inhabitants sculpted, transported across the island and erected.

Between AD 1000 and 1600, the islanders carved about 900 statues, chipping them out of an ancient volcano with stone tools. The statues' characteristic jutting brows, elongated heads and sloping bodies give them an austere, brooding look. Some are topped with heavy headdresses called *pukao*, cylindrical sculptures made of red scoria (a rough kind of lava); this material is also used, with coral, to give the effect of deep-set eyes. The statues typically measure more than 12 feet tall, and some weigh as much as 82 tons. The islanders call the sculptures *moai* and their island Rapa Nui.

When Roggeveen arrived, he saw many of the *moai* erect on their platforms, their backs to the sea, and the natives prostrating themselves in apparent worship before the images. 'These stone figures caused us to be filled with wonder,' he wrote in his log, 'for we could not understand how it was possible that people who are destitute of heavy or thick timber, and also of stout cordage, out of which to construct gear, had been able to erect them.'

His crew put their minds at ease when they wrongly 'discovered' that the statues were made of packed clay.

Fifty-two years later, Captain James Cook, after sailing south from New Zealand to avoid tropical currents and trade winds and weathering treacherous Antarctic blizzards and rough seas, became the second European to visit Rapa Nui. He recognized the *moai* as 'hewn stones' and wrote of the *ahu*, or platforms, on which they stood: 'The workmanship is not inferior to the best plain piece of masonry we have in England. They use no sort of cement; yet the joints are exceedingly close, and the stones morticed and tenanted [sic] one into another, in a very artful manner.' Cook also articulated the puzzle that remains unsolved to this day: 'We could hardly conceive how these islanders, wholly unacquainted with any mechanical power, could raise such stupendous figures, and afterwards place the large cylindric stones upon their heads.'

Cook observed, however, that the islanders no longer worshipped the *moai*. They also no longer sculpted them, or even bothered to preserve or mend the ones

that existed. If he had travelled inland, he would have found a startling sight: *moai* littered along paths like the discarded playthings of giants; others buried in soil up to their necks; and hundreds more in the quarry where they were sculpted, unfinished and abandoned.

In the centuries since, a wave of expeditions has washed over the island, as explorers, archaeologists and anthropologists have grappled with unanswered questions. Who were the original Rapanui? How and why did they carve, transport and erect their monolithic *moai*? And what happened to dissolve a civilization once unified enough to turn a mountain into a gallery of statues?

The NOVA team arriving during Easter week, 1998, hopes to shed some light on some of these questions by tackling the challenges of transporting and raising a *moai*, *pukao* and all, using only stone, wood, rope and human strength. Three groups of scientists and seventy volunteers have come together in a four-week effort to match wits with the ancients. They have enlisted the help of local artists and sculptors and a crew of local workers. It is a combustible mix of participants, but their frictions are overshadowed by a common goal: to succeed where others have failed in demonstrating a viable, efficient and historically accurate method.

Jo Anne Van Tilburg heads the first part of the project: to build a model *moai* and show how it might have been moved. An archaeologist at UCLA, she has been studying the Rapanui people and their *moai* for fifteen years. She has struggled to understand what the *moai* meant to their creators, tracing a tenuous thread of tradition and oral history passed down through chaotic times.

'The answer is deeply embedded in the culture, and much of that answer, unfortunately, has been lost,' Van Tilburg notes. She adds simply, 'The meaning of the *moai* to me, as an outsider, is family. The *moai* is their ancestor. It's the link with the past.'

Recently, Van Tilburg has been tackling the more concrete question of how the early Rapanui got the *moai* from the quarry to their platforms, or *ahu*, a journey of as much as 10 miles. Rapanui folklore has it that the *moai* were moved by *mana*, or divine power. Those who possessed *mana* were said to be able to command the *moai* to move. According to oral history, the *moai* 'walked' to their final resting spots. Like other archaeologists before her, Van Tilburg is sure there must be a more practical explanation.

Indeed, the mystery is not *that* the Rapanui were able to move the *moai*. After all, there are plenty of ways to roll, drag or even 'walk' the *moai* upright across the island — even if the choices are limited by prehistoric technology. The question is exactly *how* they did it. And the only way to find out, Van Tilburg believes, is to get out in the field and try it.

Van Tilburg has spent years preparing for this experiment at home in Los Angeles, using computer simulations. First, she and her husband, architect Jan Van Tilburg, measured all of the nearly 900 *moai* and mapped the contours of the island and its ancient roads. She then enlisted the help of Zvi Shiller, a professor of mechanical and aerospace engineering at UCLA who works on robotics, motion planning and intelligent vehicles. With the Van Tilburgs' data, Shiller was able to create on his computer a model of a statistically average *moai* and a virtual Rapa Nui. The scientists would use these models to develop their plan.

'I find it very useful to incorporate graphics into my work,' says Shiller, sitting in his Los Angeles office and peering through his spectacles at his computer screen, on which Rapa Nui appears as a swirl of coloured pixels, complete with slopes, rocks and footpaths. 'It's often difficult to interpret cold numbers. With one look on this screen, however, you can see if a particular path for moving the *moai* makes sense or not.'

Shiller points out that a similar technology was used for planning the motions of the Pathfinder on Mars. 'And you know,' he says with characteristic humour, 'the comparison is appropriate, because there are people who think the *moai* on Easter Island were moved by extraterrestrials.'

Jo Anne Van Tilburg and Shiller sit together in front of the computer as he shows her what his program can do. He taps a few keys, and a *moai* icon begins to move along a path. Van Tilburg smiles as she watches years of research come to fruition on the little electronic island. Immediately, though, she and Shiller begin debating the efficiency of different paths. The computer juggles such variables as the difficulty of the path, the number of people needed to move the *moai*, and the time it would take. Their goal is to identify the most energy-optimal path. One path requires fewer people but more time; another is more direct but steeper and so requires more manpower. The computer also takes into account the ease of transporting food and water to various paths.

Moving 900 *moai* gave the Rapanui plenty of opportunities for trial and error, Shiller notes. Decades of experimentation, he says, must have led the Rapanui to an efficient solution.

'They probably tried every path and every transportation method possible for them,' he points out. 'It's my guess that over time they probably converged on a similar solution to what our computer did in a few minutes here.' If the NOVA team can figure out the most efficient method of moving the *moai*, he argues, they will have solved the mystery.

Shiller cautions, however, that the computer can only take numerical information into account. 'When you go to the real site and do the experiment, only then do you learn how you should have modified your original model. We really don't know what kind of path they took.'

In the end, Van Tilburg and Shiller figure that the Rapanui had plenty of time but perhaps limited manpower. The computer finds a path that requires only fifty people for most of the journey, and up to seventy in short stretches that are steep.

'This is it!' says Shiller, as he moves the *moai* icon along a slope. 'Look, you can actually see the view – the mountain on the right, then you reach the top of the hump, and then you see the whole sea in front of you.'

A few months later, Van Tilburg and Shiller stand together on Rapa Nui. From its highest point, Maunga (Mount) Terevaka, they can feast on a 360-degree view: nothing but ocean and clouds, a full circle of horizon. The peak stands 1500 feet above sea level and 10,000 feet from the base of the land massif at the bottom of the ocean. After a day and a night of rain, the air is fresh and clear, but winds buffet the visitors from every direction. The roads are rivers of mud, but the black volcanic debris strewn over the grassy terrain makes detours impossible.

Back at sea level, Van Tilburg watches as members of the NOVA team pour concrete into a fibreglass mould. The first step in the process of moving and raising a *moai* is to build their own (to avoid damaging an original *moai*), using the computer model Shiller developed in Los Angeles. Team member Darus Ane has constructed the mould, based on Shiller's specifications. A native Hawaiian with a passion for the study of ancient Polynesian voyaging, Ane is an accomplished watersports athlete who helped found the Long Beach (CA) Kahakai Outrigger Canoe Club. He works as a firefighter in Los Angeles.

Ane oversees team members and local workers as they pour a specially brewed concrete into the mould (using the original material in the quarry would have been too time consuming). When it cures, this mixture of red scoria, sand, cement and

Workers prepare the ahu *on which the NOVA team will erect its* moai. Ahu Tongariki, *the largest* ahu *on the island, stands in the background. In 1960, a tidal wave toppled the fifteen Tongariki* moai; *they were restored in the mid-1990s under the direction of Claudio Cristino.*

A traditional Polynesian double canoe, called a Waka. This kind of double-canoe design is believed to have been used by the first Polynesians to settle Easter Island.

aggregate will replicate the density, texture and colour of the material from which real *moai* were carved. The mixture must cure for several days. In the meantime, NOVA team members turn their attention to building a model *ahu* for the *moai* at Tongariki, the site of the largest *ahu* on the island. This is where the second and third stages of the experiment – placing the *pukao* and raising the *moai* – will take place.

Three days later, Van Tilburg declares, 'Gentlemen, I want it cut!' Workers take a chain saw to the fibreglass mould and the 4-metre-tall, 9.5-ton *moai* is born. The entire team, watching, lets out a cheer. Van Tilburg's voice is the loudest. She has nurtured this baby from its conception on the computer screen to its delivery from the fibreglass womb.

'People call me the mother of the *moai*,' she says as she admires the statue. 'And right now I feel very fond of that object. I can see how people would invest family histories and family traditions in something like this.'

The next day, local sculptors Santi Hito and Cristian Pakarati finish the *moai* by carving its face. Hito, a native of Rapa Nui who now works in the California film industry, also serves as the NOVA team's translator. That night, at the Hotel Otai in the island's only town, Hanga Roa, the team meets to discuss strategy.

Most experts agree that the original *moai*-movers must have used some sort of wooden sledge. Since the *moai* were sculpted before they were transported, dragging them directly along the ground would have caused unacceptable damage. In 1955 Norwegian archaeologist Thor Heyerdahl tied a 10-ton *moai* to a sledge made from a tree fork and 180 islanders helped him pull it a few yards over the sand. Although they succeeded in moving the *moai*, it took so many people that the method seemed impractical: it would have taken 1500 people, for example, to move Paro, the island's heaviest *moai*.

Heyerdahl's colleague William Mulloy returned in 1960 and tried a different approach. He fashioned a vertical A-frame, like two legs of a tripod, from which he suspended a horizontal, Y-shaped sledge. The *moai* Paro was placed face-down on the sledge, with its belly fitting in the curve of the Y. Protected by the sledge, the *moai*'s belly acted as a fulcrum or balance point, allowing the legs of the A-frame to be tipped forward in alternating steps, bipedal fashion. Using this method, Mulloy

Members of Thor Heyerdahl's 1986 expedition attempt to 'walk' a moai *upright, using ropes to rock it from side to side.*

was able to move the largest *moai* using only ninety people. But the method was complex, required large trees, and placed stress on the statue's neck. Moreover, the frame would not have balanced properly for statues that did not have protruding bellies.

In 1986 Heyerdahl tried again, this time with the help of Czech archaeologist Pavel Pavel. Listening more literally to the legend of *moai* 'walking', they attached four ropes to an upright *moai*, and twenty pullers 'walked' it along, rocking it from edge to edge the way one might move a refrigerator. Although Heyerdahl and Pavel succeeded in 'walking' a *moai* along level ground for a short distance, the method seemed ill suited for long distances and steep slopes. Damage to the base of the *moai* forced them to halt the experiment.

At the Hotel Otai, Polynesian canoe expert Ted Ralston explains to the group that the lashings and crossbeams featured in Polynesian canoe design provide the inspiration for the sledge technology they will be implementing the next day. Canoe technology was essential to the survival and spread of Polynesian culture. In ancient times, outrigger canoes allowed people to travel safely from island to island. These canoes are distinguished by two beams that extend from one side of the hull. The beams stabilize the vessel and keep it from capsizing. In the larger vessels used on longer voyages, they act as crossbeams to bind two hulls together.

Van Tilburg believes that to solve the problems of transporting *moai* over land, the Rapanui simply transferred the technology they had developed for transporting goods and people over water. Accordingly, she has designed an A-frame sled that features crossbeams lashed to the frame in the same way the ancient Polynesians lashed crossbeams to the hulls of their voyaging canoes.

Her plan calls on another seafaring technology as well, as Ralston describes. 'Throughout most of Polynesia, the islands have rocky coasts with rough sea conditions heading into them. There are very few areas where there's a very good sandy approach to a harbour. So the Polynesians became very adept at getting their canoes into and out of the water over these rocky outcroppings. And the way it was traditionally done was with a canoe ladder.'

The Polynesians built wooden ladders, complete with rungs and rails, and extended them into the water. They used ropes to lower the canoes down the ladders at the beginning of a voyage, and at the end dragged their boats up the ladders on to the shore. They used similar structures to transport giant logs down the mountain to build their canoes. Often they slid their boats over fixed rails but, as Ralston points out, 'We have information from Herb Connie, our archaeologist, and from Captain Cook's journals that rollers were used on some of the heavier double canoes.'

Van Tilburg and her colleagues plan to drag the *moai*, tied to their outrigger-type A-frame, over a track built just like a canoe ladder. Considering the great weight of the *moai*, they will try the heavy-boat method using loose rollers rather than fixed cross-ties. Their design is unique in that it employs know-how that the early Rapanui would have had themselves.

In 1947 Heyerdahl and his companions sailed the Kon-Tiki, an Inca-style balsa raft, 5000 miles from Peru to Polynesia to show that Easter Island could have been settled by South Americans. The raft was named in honour of the Peruvian sun god.

'That's the key issue for us,' interjects Van Tilburg. 'Not to bring something here that just dropped in out of the sky, but to bring an idea that comes from as authentic an interpretation as we can come up with of Polynesian cultural history.'

The issue of whether or not the Rapanui were in fact Polynesian has been a source of fierce debate for much of the past hundred years. French anthropologist Alfred Métraux made an expedition to Easter Island in 1934 and was the first to conclude that the natives were exclusively Polynesian. Thor Heyerdahl, however, became convinced that although Polynesians had entered the population later, the original Rapanui were South American Indians. He believed that the trade winds and prevailing currents make it far easier to sail to Easter Island from the east than from the west.

When Heyerdahl first espoused this idea, the experts said that the precolonial South Americans could never have travelled that far in their primitive boats. So in 1947, in an early foray into experimental archaeology, Heyerdahl built a balsa raft in the style of the Incas and sailed it with five companions from Peru to Polynesia. The *Kon-Tiki* covered over 5000 miles in 101 days and, though it didn't hit Rapa Nui, it showed that it well might have.

Ancient Rapanui folklore, too, told of the island being settled by a divine king named Machaa, who 'steered in the direction of the setting sun' to find the island. Stories tell how Machaa's people, later called the Long-Ears because of their elongated earlobes, began to sculpt the *moai* about fifty years later, presumably to honour their first deceased ancestor. Then another race colonized the island, this time arriving from the west. These 'Short-Ears' helped the Long-Ears build the *moai*, but scarcity of resources led to war between the two groups. According to legend, the Short-Ears massacred the Long-Ears in a battle at Poike Ditch. After their victory, they toppled all the *moai*. To this day many Rapanui claim this legend as their history.

In Heyerdahl's estimation, the *moai* were 'characteristic of the pre-Inca period of northwestern South America'. He claimed that the *moai* were very similar to monolithic structures in Tiahuanaco, Peru, and that their type was hardly found elsewhere in Polynesia. He also asserted that the stone architecture of the island, the stone picks used to carve volcanic rock, the huts built like reed boats, the reed boats themselves, the bottle gourds, sweet potatoes, and the practice of elongating ear lobes with heavy earrings could all be traced to pre-Inca South America.

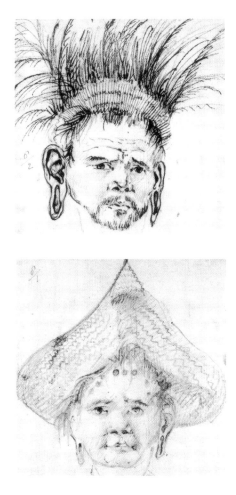

William Hodges, an artist who accompanied Cook to Easter Island in 1774, made these sketches of island natives. The man wore a head-dress of grass and feathers, and the woman a straw bonnet to protect her from the sun. Both used perforation to elongate their earlobes.

Heyerdahl's notions coincided nicely with native myths; he also had a charismatic presence, a romantic life story, and a series of best-selling books describing his endeavours and conclusions. By 1989, when he published *Easter Island: The Mystery Solved*, he had succeeded in persuading the general public of his ideas. His professional colleagues, however, have been less impressed.

The Rapa Nui Archaeological Survey, a Chilean—American co-operative effort that began in 1968 and continues today, dismantled Heyerdahl's argument point by point. Seeking a comprehensive description of the island, the survey

archaeologists have sketched, mapped and measured 19,000 items, including 240 *ahu*, 886 *moai*, 2536 earth ovens and 3224 house foundations. They found that the *ahu* were more similar to stone altars common throughout Polynesia than they were to the ruins of Tiahuanaco. Heyerdahl had postulated that the South Americans had brought the reed plant with them, but pollen analysis showed that the reeds used in the reed boats had been growing on Easter Island for more than 30,000 years, while the island was settled some time between AD 400 and 750. Excavations at Poike Ditch unearthed no mass of human remains to suggest a great battle having taken place there. On the other hand, skeletal remains that have been excavated from various sites on the island show definite Polynesian characteristics.

Heyerdahl's voyage on the *Kon-Tiki* was a great feat, and it showed what was possible. But it fell short of proving his thesis. In 1976 a group of Pacific islanders, organized by University of Hawaii anthropologist Ben Finney, sailed a replica of a traditional double canoe from Hawaii to Tahiti and back, proving that the Polynesians were equally capable of reaching Easter Island.

The Polynesians of the first millennium were great sea voyagers and often set sail to the east, against the trade winds, in search of new lands. Over the centuries, they migrated to and populated Tahiti, the Marquesas Islands, Hawaii and New Zealand. By contrast, the South American Indians had no history of long-distance sea voyages. And most anthropologists agree that the linguistic, cultural and genetic evidence shows that though they could have drifted with the winds to Rapa

Nui, they didn't. The professional consensus: the original Rapanui were Polynesians.

Jo Anne Van Tilburg stands in front of Rano Raraku, the quarry that served as the site of the Rapanui's *moai*-carving 'factory'. Here the Rapanui sculpted their statues out of hardened volcanic ash. She gestures towards the slopes scattered with toppled and half-carved *moai*. Some are still tethered to the rocky face of the mountain, sightless faces tilted towards the sky. Others have fallen where they stood and lie half-buried in the drifted earth of centuries. 'More than half the statues on the island are still in the quarry here,' she says. 'The question naturally arises whether they were meant to stay here.'

Katharine Routledge discovered the extent of the quarry in 1914. She was an Englishwoman and member of the Royal Cruising Club who had set sail on a streamlined twin-masted yacht with the support of the British Admiralty, the Royal Society, the British Association, the Royal Geographical Society and England's leading Pacific-island anthropologists. She spent sixteen months ashore, often alone with one crew member among the 250 Rapanui, while her ship sailed elsewhere, returning only periodically. She made meticulous notes on the people,

Moai lie scattered along the quarry hillside. Some lie on their backs, still tethered to the mountain by stone keels.

their customs and language, and of course the *moai*. Her journals and the book she published in 1919 have been an inspiration to Easter Island researchers.

A member of the 1914 expedition led by Katharine Routledge poses next to one of the island's moai.

At Rano Raraku, Routledge discovered that more than half the *moai* on the island were still in the quarry area. She noticed that none of these statues had eyes, while all the *moai* that had fallen from their *ahu* did. Apparently the eyes were carved and inserted just before the statues were set in position. Scattered around the quarry were *toki* – picks made of basalt, a harder rock than the volcanic tuff of the mountainside. The variously unfinished *moai*, some still untethered from the mountain, taught her much about the method of sculpting.

The artists began by chipping directly into the mountainside, outlining the profile, creating the figure face up. Eventually, when the front and sides were finished, the *moai* was attached only by its downward-facing back, which was shaped like the keel of a boat. Only then did the workers separate the *moai* from its volcanic womb and begin to move it down from the quarry. By studying the various states of the backs of the statues that she found standing upright in the dirt, she concluded that the backs were finished while in this position, before transportation to the *ahu*.

But why were hundreds of *moai* left unfinished, standing half-buried in the earth or suspended in mid-gestation in the quarry? What could have caused this isolated, apparently highly organized society to collapse and abandon the work of centuries?

While the legend of the Long-Ears and the Short-Ears may be fictional, it appears that some sort of strife occurred among the Rapanui. Certainly, by the seventeenth century, the '*moai* cult' was disintegrating. The most likely reason was the increasing scarcity of forests, tillable land and food.

Lush forests once covered this windswept island. By analysing ancient pollen, scientists have determined that a species of palm tree called *Jubaea chilensis* flourished here at the time the first inhabitants arrived. Long before the island was first sighted by Europeans, however, the forests had disappeared. 'Nature has been exceedingly sparing of her favours to this spot,' wrote Captain Cook.

One cause of environmental degradation may have been the *moai* industry, which required great amounts of wood for sledges. (Canoes and canoe ladders, of course, also required wood.) Today, the *Jubaea chilensis* palm trees have vanished. Eucalyptus groves planted by the Chilean government provide most of the island's wood.

With the *moai* siphoning off much of the island's resources, tribes rebelled, toppling and decapitating the great statues. Nothing could bring back the forests and the fields denuded by overpopulation, however; the people turned to caves for shelter and tending small gardens for sustenance. There is evidence that famine even led some to cannibalism.

The arrival of 'civilized' visitors hardly helped matters. Beginning in 1805, the Rapanui suffered half a century of slave raids by North and South American traders. These culminated in 1862 with the Great Peruvian Slave Raid. Eight Peruvian ships happened to meet at Easter Island with the same purpose in mind. They banded together and managed to capture more than 200 people, including the royal family of King Kaimakoi and nearly all the leading figures of Rapa Nui.

In response to pressure from the Catholic bishop of Tahiti and the French minister in Lima, the Peruvian government eventually ordered the return of all 1000 Rapanui now in captivity, but the effort was in vain. Ninety per cent of them died before the return journey, and most of the remaining hundred died of smallpox on the voyage back. The fifteen surviving slaves brought the smallpox home with them, and before long the entire island population had sunk to 111 desperate souls. The era of aboriginal culture on Rapa Nui was over.

From a bountiful civilization with the resources and the leadership to build nearly a thousand monolithic statues, the Rapanui had been reduced to a handful of wary cave dwellers. Between 1866 and 1871, missionaries led by a Frenchman named Eugène Eyraud managed to convert the islanders to Christianity and brought new crops and livestock to the depleted landscape. The necessary casualties, of course, were the last vestiges of native culture. In 1888 Chile annexed the island that nobody wanted, and Easter Island commenced its twentieth-century incarnation as a provider of quaint figurines carved by natives.

This was the Easter Island that Katharine Routledge encountered in 1914. In the months that she camped out at Rano Raraku quarry, among the fallen giants of more prosperous times, she spent much of her energies trying to figure out the greatest mystery of the Rapanui: how did they transport these monoliths across miles of rugged countryside?

Some Rapanui still believe the *moai* were 'walked' to their destinations. At the Hotel Otai meeting, an argument erupts between the native members of the NOVA team and the visiting scientists. Sergio Rapu, a Rapanui archaeologist, argues that the bases of the *moai* at Rano Raraku were intentionally curved to allow the *moai* to be rocked from side to side. The bases flaked as the *moai* were rocked back and forth. It is the same point that Heyerdahl made in 1986.

Claudio Cristino, the NOVA team member who will lead the *moai*-raising phase of the experiment, suggests that the curved base was a feature designed for raising the *moai*, not walking it. A professor of prehistory at the University of Chile, Cristino has been Easter Island's resident archaeologist for the past two decades and directs the Rapa Nui Archaeological Survey. Santi Hito, however, insists that the *moai* were transported vertically and as proof points to the fact that the heads have fallen far from the bodies along the paths.

Van Tilburg suggests that some *moai* may have been erected at the side of the road for some reason. Many of the *moai* found lying along the paths are much larger than the ones on *ahu*, and she hypothesizes that they may have been too large to drag across the island to an *ahu*. The facts that these *moai* are decorated with carvings and that bowls and other ceremonial artefacts have been excavated around them suggest to her that they were used for religious purposes right there for years.

The scientists turn to Raphael Rapu, an esteemed local artist and sculptor who is descended from a long line of Rapanui carvers, and ask which way he would move it if he were in charge of the task. Rapu is the foreman of the local crew assisting the NOVA team. Rapu and Hito engage in a short conversation in the Rapanui language.

'He could move it either way,' translates Hito. 'It depends.'

Later, some of the group continue the conversation as they walk up the transport road. 'The *moai* were probably moved in different ways,' suggests Sergio Rapu. 'And of those that walked, some walked with protective frames, so they have no damage on the bottom, and others walked without frames.'

'Well, then,' Van Tilburg counters, 'look over your shoulder at that slope, and let's imagine how *moai* walked up that slope. I can't picture it.'

'Yeah, me either,' Cristino chimes in.

'I agree,' Rapu concedes, beginning to laugh. 'That's one mystery we'll preserve. I tell you, this whole Easter Island mystery is hard. I'm going to write a book: *Easter Island, the Mystery Unsolved.*'

A few days later, the NOVA team assembles on the beautiful plain of Tongariki, close to the Rano Raraku quarry on the eastern part of the island. The model *moai* and sledge have been placed here, between the quarry and the model *ahu*, by crane. On this bright, sunny April morning, after years of meticulous planning, Van Tilburg and her colleagues are going to try to move the *moai*.

As they did for Thor Heyerdahl in 1955, some of the Rapanui conduct a traditional Polynesian ceremony, called an *umu tahu*, to ensure the success of the enterprise. A Catholic priest, as the missionary Eyraud would have been glad to see, also blesses the project.

The concrete statue lies face up on Van Tilburg's A-frame sledge, lashed to it tightly with rope. The sledge, in turn, lies at the beginning of a sort of canoe-ladder track, with thin eucalyptus logs lying across it that will act as rollers. According to the original plan, the *moai* would have lain free of straps, relying only on its own weight for stability. But after hearty argument among the team members, Van Tilburg has agreed to the rope lashings. They are genuine canoe lashings, used since prehistoric times.

The team also debated whether to use rollers rather than dragging the sledge over fixed cross-ties. They have decided to try the rollers first, since they had worked well in a trial run in Los Angeles. Rollers should make sliding easier, as long as the sledge is stable.

Attached to the sledge are five ropes for pulling: two long ones in front for the main thrust, one on each side to keep it from sliding, and one more in the back to act as a sort of rudder. Twelve workers on each rope make a total of sixty people in the pulling force.

The scientists are ready to go, but the sixty Rapanui workers are busy in a group meeting, led by Niko Haoa, a local entrepreneur and outfitter whose family has lived on Rapa Nui for many generations. After a while, Haoa comes over and reports: 'They want a raise because, you know, there'll probably be an accident, and who's going to cover for that?' The scene illustrates a difficulty that must have faced the ancient *moai*-creators as well. They too had to manage their workers, keeping them happy while extracting an enormous amount of labour from them.

Finally, the negotiations reach a satisfactory conclusion and the pullers take their positions. According to a last-minute brainstorm, some of the pulling crew will use levers to keep the rollers in line between thrusts. As they get ready to heave ho, someone asks Vince Lee, a Wyoming architect and expert in Inca stonework and stone-moving who has been enlisted as an adviser to the NOVA team, if the thing is going to roll.

'You bet,' he says. 'With all these people on it, it can't help but roll. The thing is, we're pulling on terrain that's flat as a pancake here. But to be valid, it's got to be something that would work going up hills and down hills and sideways on hills. I think this system would be a little harder to do on that kind of terrain, but let's give them a chance and see what happens.'

Ironically, this is the same objection Van Tilburg has raised to Heyerdahl's 1986 experiment 'walking' the *moai* – that it would never work on hills. Later in the expedition, she will have her chance to test her rig on a slope.

But now Haoa walks to the front of the *moai* and shouts a countdown in Rapanui. On cue, the crew heaves, the ropes draw taut as steel and, slowly but inexorably, the *moai* begins to move. A crowd of local enthusiasts, swelled by tourists who have become more interested in the experiment than in the genuine ancient *moai* on the island, cheers and claps, urging the men on. Their exertion slides the statue about 2 metres down the track before they rest.

The lever men straighten out the rollers, which have skewed like a defective Venetian blind.

'It slides, it doesn't roll!' someone yells.

'Well, we rolled a bit,' Cristino replies. But he points out that if the rollers tend to get stuck, going up or down slopes is going to be a problem. 'Maybe rollers are not the best solution,' he suggests. 'Fixing the rollers in the frame and just dragging it on top, even with no lubricants – water would do the trick – would probably be easier.'

The pulling team strains to move the moai forward as it lies face-up on the sledge.

Lee agrees that dragging the sledge across fixed cross beams now looks like a better idea. Using lubricants – sweet potatoes, for example – would be more efficient than having to stop and reset the rollers with levers. 'Rollers always look so good on paper,' he says, 'because on paper you can imagine a perfectly flat surface and perfectly straight, cylindrical rollers, but in the real world, out in the boondocks, it's real hard to do. An experiment like this is such a perfect example of the contrast between doing something on paper and actually trying to do it in the real world.'

The NOVA team decides to use a crane to lift the sledge so workers can get underneath to lash the rolling logs to the rails. Later that day, they are ready to try again. Using the fixed rollers, it works like a charm – that is, if you can call pulling a 9.5-ton *moai* 100 metres in four hours working like a charm. If the ancient Rapanui had anything, however, it was plenty of time.

Everyone is quite cheered by this change in fortune. 'We have successfully moved this *moai* a greater distance than anyone has ever done before,' Van Tilburg says afterwards, 'so that is exciting. And we're going to go even further.'

Lee is still wondering how the system will work on sloping ground, but Cristino is not worried about it. 'Not a problem,' he says. 'You just put on more people. With a 15 per cent slope, you will need double this number of people.'

What about lumpy ground? asks Lee. 'All these individual logs would have to be supported somehow,' he points out. 'Otherwise, the minute the weight comes down on them, they're going to go down into the depression.'

'Yeah, but if you follow the traditional, ancient roads, most of the distance they're very smooth,' Cristino answers.

Lee now raises another issue. Since the *moai* all stood facing inland, wouldn't it be more logical to transport the *moai* in a face-down position, base first? Then, when you reached the *ahu*, you could simply raise the *moai* directly into position. To do that with the *moai* face up, you would have to approach the *ahu* base first, from the back, or ocean, side. But most of the *ahu* are so close to the shore that that would be impossible. In order to erect a *moai* from a face-up position, you would either have to slide the base backwards as you raised the head or somehow lift the *moai*, flip it on to its face, and rotate it into a base-first position.

'Absolutely,' Cristino agrees. 'You have three extra movements that you can avoid. It would take more work to build the wooden frame for a face-down position, but it's not a problem.'

'You do it once,' Lee puts in, 'and it's done for all time.'

'It is also in keeping with the evidence we have,' Cristino continues. 'That is, most of the statues were abandoned face down, and all the evidence indicates they were put face down when they were taken out of the quarry.'

Van Tilburg is less concerned with this issue. Some statues were abandoned face up, some face down, she says, and neither case is proof that the *moai* were transported that way. 'Over longer distances, the face-up method might be preferred because it might be safer. From my point of view, either position would work with this rig.'

The next day, it's back to work. There's more yardage to be covered, this time going up a gentle slope. The pullers – now forty people, including some women – take position, Haoa chants his cadence, and they begin to move the *moai*. The giant moves more slowly this time, straining against gravity, but it moves. 'There you go,' says Cristino, smiling. 'Fabulous,' Lee laughs. He is becoming a convert to the method. 'I think we need a race now. We set two tracks here and have a drag race with two *moai*. See who gets to the *ahu* first.'

It's a moment of vindication for Van Tilburg and her sledge, and she is beside herself. 'The enthusiasm, the excitement, the co-ordination,' she says, 'and the people have fully taken over everything. They're making all the decisions together. What we know now,' she adds, 'is that we can go up hill and down dale with this. It's very flexible. And the width of this track and of this *moai* with its frame is almost exactly the width of the ancient ramps.'

A casual observer might lose track of the importance of compatibility with ancient history, but it is never far from the minds of the scientific team. As the last of the afternoon light comes slanting over the hills, and the pulling crew,

Moving the *moai* up the ramp

1. Using ropes and levers.

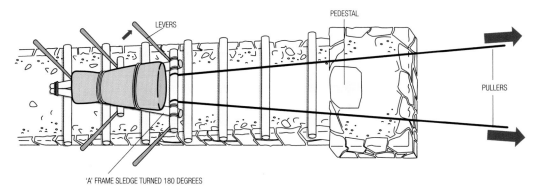

PEDESTAL

LEVERS

PULLERS

'A' FRAME SLEDGE TURNED 180 DEGREES

sunburned and exhausted, has gone home for a well-deserved supper, canoe expert Ralston and Van Tilburg reflect on the relevance of their technique.

'We've simply transferred technology from another Polynesian industry, canoe building,' she says. 'Polynesian people would have known how to do this, no question. It's an indigenous concept, and it works like a charm.'

'There's thousands of years of history in the Polynesian voyaging canoes,' adds Ralston, 'and this is the same basic structure. The two semi-parallel beams allow the weight of the *moai* to nestle in the middle, and it's stabilized very much like an outrigger canoe. The structure's quite flexible, and these lashings are very strong and flexible. They allow the frame to accommodate and twist as the ground changes. It's a very compliant system all the way around. We also used the *keke* [an ancient Polynesian tool] to get the lashings nice and tight.'

'We're not reinventing the wheel here,' says Van Tilburg. 'We're doing something that's right out of Polynesian history.'

'This technology has been around for 10,000 years, all over the Pacific,' Ralston confirms. 'All we did – and what we think they did – was transfer it from ocean to land.'

The next day is May Day, and the NOVA team is going to try to accomplish the next phase of *moai* transportation: moving it up a ramp to the base of its *ahu*. Rapu, the sculptor, and his local crew constructed it to match the proportions of the *ahu* at Ahu Akivi – its 4-by-7-metre platform is the appropriate size for their 10-ton *moai*.

Rapu and his men have also prepared a ramp of stones leading up to their *ahu*. To get statues from ground level up to the level of the base of the *ahu*, the ancients built ramps constructed from the virtually limitless supply of lava stones. Ruins of these ramps can still be found around the island. Presumably the islanders dragged the *moai* up the ramps base first, and then tilted them up from there on to their *ahu*.

Jan and Jo Anne Van Tilburg are at opposite ends of the ramp, measuring heights and determining the slope their *moai* will have to traverse. The *ahu* is 1.3 metres high, and the *moai* is now resting at the base of the ramp, 20 metres away. 'We divide 1 metre 30 by 20 metres,' Jan Van Tilburg says, 'and we have a six and a half per cent slope.'

Vince Lee and Zvi Shiller have each measured the slope themselves, and they both estimate it at 3.45 per cent. But the Van Tilburgs are unperturbed. 'Six and a half per cent,' Jan repeats. 'That's a challenging slope. But it's a challenge that the ancients must have had to meet every time they raised a statue.'

One challenge that the ancients also had to face, if they transported the *moai* face up, was to turn it over and around before going up the ramp. But that ancient challenge is one the NOVA team is going to avoid. They bring in a crane to do the job.

Lee is a bit disappointed with a strategy that relies on modern technology at key moments. 'It's just a shame to see all the tricky parts done with the crane,' he complains. 'I mean, doing this with manpower would be somewhat of a project.' But, as Jan Van Tilburg explains, they are facing time constraints and really have no choice at this point. Even using the crane, it takes most of a morning to reposition the *moai*, as the experts tend to every nuance of the machine's moves like a team of doctors overseeing robotic surgery.

The next thing the team needs to do is set up a track on the ramp. They place eucalyptus logs across the ramp, spaced like a series of railroad ties, then lubricate them with banana stumps and water. The sixty pullers move the *moai* right up the slope within minutes. Most of the way, that is.

The final 2 metres presents a challenge, for the slope increases sharply in that last portion. The pullers find themselves positioned behind the *ahu*, several feet below the *moai*. Fortunately, Van Tilburg has decided to set the *moai* on an inland *ahu*; if the *ahu* were situated on the shore, it would drop off right into the sea, and the pullers would have fallen into the water. But even with firm ground to stand on, the final 2 metres are still a challenge.

2. Using a lever beam for mechanical advantage.

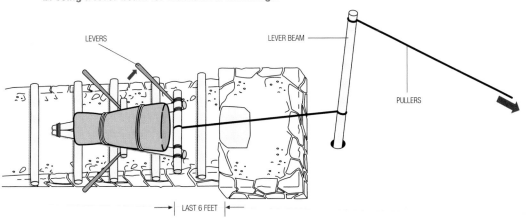

LEVERS

LEVER BEAM

PULLERS

LAST 6 FEET

The NOVA team decides to try a different approach for this final bit. They tie the rope from the sledge to a large lever, and a reduced crew of twenty people, working behind the *ahu*, pulls on the lever beam. In this way, although they have to pull 4 feet to move the sledge 1 foot, they pull with four times as much force per person. Twenty people will pull with the strength of eighty.

Jo Anne Van Tilburg watches with satisfaction as the *moai* crawls up the last few feet. 'It's a good method,' she says.

'I was waiting for something to break,' says Shiller.

'Well, we were all waiting for it. We needed a stronger beam. But it worked!'

Setting up the lever and moving the final 2 metres has taken all day, but the team has finally brought the 'feet' of the *moai* to the edge of the *ahu*. The long process that has drawn these archaeologists and anthropologists from around the world has brought the ten-ton statue to the brink of its final resting place. And it has also begun to abrade some nerves.

Cristino is in charge of raising and crowning the *moai*. And in his opinion some modifications need to be made in the sledge before they can begin raising it. For one thing, he wants to cut off the ends of the protruding logs, which might get in the way. He also wants to retie the rig for stability. But Van Tilburg feels that this is still her baby, and she's not about to see Cristino interfere with years of planning. She's also understandably impatient to reach the finish line after coming so close. Cristino tells her they need to take a full day to make his modifications.

'I'm telling you we probably don't have to do that. It's going to go up, Claudio.'

'That's not what Raphael told me.'

'I don't know what he's telling you. This thing's going to go up, and it's going to go up with the method we all agreed to. There's nobody, including you, who's going to step in there tomorrow and change everything around. It's too late!'

But Cristino's prudence wins out, and his crew takes an extra day to rearrange the *moai* on the rig and cut off the protruding ends of the logs – with a chain saw, not an ancient basalt axe.

In the meantime, Lee has been working on another experiment. As he is quick to point out, he is not an expert on Rapa Nui: 'I didn't know a thing about this place until two weeks ago.' But he is an expert on the Incas and how they might have moved their giant statues, and the entire time he has been watching the workers drag the Van Tilburg sledge along, the problem of elevating and rotating the *moai* has been getting under his skin. Like a good architect, he has built a small wooden model of a sledge he would like to see tested. On the hood of the team pickup truck, he demonstrates how it would work.

'Watching them, it occurred to me that an improvement would be a sledge which has lots of cross-bars on it,' he says, 'so that you have many places to apply leverage. That would enable you to get this sledge up on to the platform here just using levers.'

The lever, Lee points out, was one of the first tools humans learned how to use. It multiplies the force of an individual's muscle power. 'If one person can pull with one hundred pounds of force,' he explains, 'the lever allows that person to apply four or five hundred pounds of force.'

Levering the sledge forward works almost like paddling a canoe, echoing the application of seafaring technology to land transport. It fits in perfectly with Van Tilburg's philosophy. And the nautical analogy doesn't end there. As Lee points out, Polynesian canoes had sails for crossing long distances over the open sea and paddles for negotiating the tight turns in harbour. In the same way, they might have used a crowd of pullers with ropes for long distances and levers for fine-tuning the final approach. Lee's sledge design would work particularly well for rotating the *moai*: the workers on one side need simply lever forward while those on the other side lever back.

'I showed this design to Raphael Rapu a couple of days ago, and he just said, *"Venga!"* [Come!],' Lee continues eagerly. 'And I followed him over to his truck, and he opened the glove compartment and pulled out some drawings he had done which are nearly identical to what I have come up with.'

Lee builds his sledge from some leftover poles and cord. Both are thinner than he would like, and there are only half as many ladder rungs and cross bars as his design calls for, but he figures it will be good enough for the 3-ton rock Rapu is supplying for the effort.

Unfortunately, when the rock arrives on the final day of the film shoot, it turns out to weigh at least 6 tons. As it lies on the sledge, visibly straining the wood's limits, Lee and Rapu assemble twelve men around the sledge. On Rapu's count, they heave on their levers, and the enormous stone inches grudgingly forward. Van Tilburg and Shiller watch with some scepticism.

'I like the levers,' Shiller comments. 'But the disadvantage is that the motions are very small. With pulling, you can actually pull 20 metres in one pull. Here, it will be at most a few inches at a time.'

'I agree,' says Van Tilburg. 'This is a very sound idea, with respect to the ethnography of the region. There's nothing here that Polynesians would not know how to do. But I'd try to pull it. Levering is not only inefficient, it looks like it might be dangerous. And it's damaging the frame.'

'Well, obviously, if we were just going up this road,' Lee replies, 'you would put ropes on it and put a whole mess of people out there. But the idea here is to show how you could make small movements in places where you really don't have any room for people to pull.'

Over the next two hours, Lee's crew moves the 6-ton stone all of 15 feet. Then they set out to try the rotation. Team members fit skids underneath the sledge and instruct the leverers: those on the left lever to the back, those on the right lever to the front, those in front lever to the left, and those at the back lever to the right. Slowly but surely, the rig begins to turn.

'Well,' says Cristino, 'I think it's an interesting experiment. The main problem we have is that the frame was built without knowing the weight of the

block. So it's tending to bend a lot. It's not because the method doesn't work; it's simply because they were not given enough time.'

Van Tilburg seems to disagree. 'The bottom line here,' she says, 'is it's not really demonstrating very much, because the design of the frame is so inadequate that we can't really make a just extrapolation from what we're seeing.'

'You know,' says Lee, 'we are moving it with twelve guys, and it's a big rock. I could hardly claim that because of that it's a successful experiment. But we've learned a whole lot of stuff. And I think we've shown that a small gang of people with levers can move a big rock. If you figure this thing weighs about 6 tons, we've got twelve guys on it now, so each guy is moving 1000 pounds of rock right now, each individual man. That's not too bad.'

'Can I make another point?' Van Tilburg interjects. 'I would say that to turn the *moai* on the frame we designed doesn't require the intricate ladder that we have here. We could have done it in a simpler way.'

'Yes,' says Shiller. 'The A-frame was just as good for the rotation part.'

'It's actually better,' Van Tilburg adds.

'Did you do it with the A-frame?' asks Lee.

'We could,' she says.

'But you didn't?' he persists.

'We didn't.'

'You used a crane for it, if I recall correctly.'

'We did exactly what the experiment required,' says Van Tilburg flatly.

'It's easy to say your sledge is perfect for it, but if you don't do it–' Lee is growing heated. 'You can call it poorly designed, if you want, but you have forty people moving 9 tons. I've got twelve people moving 6 tons. If you're trying to move an 80-ton rock, you better make most use of your people.'

When he gets home, Lee will try to prove his point by testing his design properly. In a friend's masonry yard in Brighton, Colorado, he has amassed a collection of large stones for the purpose of learning how the ancient Incas might have moved their own statues. Spurred by the memory of his ill-equipped Easter Island experiment, he will attempt to kill two birds with one monolithic stone.

On 15 December 1998 he meets his friend and thirty volunteers at the masonry yard to try his lever sledge again. This time, his equipment has been properly built to specification: the sturdy sledge measures 10 by 15 feet and its wooden ladder 'road' is built of four 5- by 10-foot sections. The ladder will be laid on a stone ramp which, although built as a replica of that at the Inca fortress at Ollantaytambo, is also similar to at least one surviving ramp on Easter Island. It is 55 feet long and rises to a 70-inch-high platform, with an average slope of 11 per cent; along one 10-foot-long section the slope increases to an intimidating 25 per cent. The stone Lee plans to move up this angle weighs 13 tons.

Lee's goal is to move the rock up the ramp and then rotate it 90 degrees, to champion his method as both the best way to get a *moai* onto its *ahu* and also as a way to solve the rotation problem.

Things start smoothly enough, as a crew of eight people, standing on top of the rock, lever the sledge easily over level ground. Because they are up high, using longer levers, each person is able to exert about 700 pounds of force, or seven times their natural power.

'Putting people on top of the load was extremely effective,' Lee recalls afterwards. 'The advantage of longer levers definitely makes up for the added weight. It seems to me it would be very helpful to have the leverers on top of the *moai* as well. Since the *moai* itself is a rounded and finished piece of work, maybe the Rapanui built a sledge all the way around the *moai* and stood on the sledge with great long levers. Then guys on ground would replace the levers each time they had to be moved.'

As his team approaches steeper parts of the ramp, Lee adds leverers; at the steepest grade, twenty-six people are working, some on top with long levers and others down below with short levers. In between forward thrusts, two 'brakemen' jam their levers to prevent backsliding.

The Sisyphus Project is an unqualified success. In two hours, Lee's team moves the 13-ton rock up the ramp to the platform and rotates it 90 degrees. Lee has moved a larger stone than Van Tilburg's, faster, up a steeper ramp, with fewer

Back in Colorado, Lee demonstrates his method for levering a heavy weight up an incline and rotating it. Placing crew members on top of the block gives them greater leverage.

workers. And his method could be applied on seacoast as well as inland *ahu*. After the frustration of his attempt on Rapa Nui, Lee's success in Colorado is especially gratifying.

Back on Rapa Nui, however, Lee's side experiment has added new frictions to the already heated debates among the team's scientists. They are beginning to seem like salesmen pitching their own sledge designs. It's not the first time during the project that critical argument has given way to squabbling. These same kinds of pressures may have escalated dissent among the ancient *moai* movers themselves. Combined with the social tensions generated by the destruction of the island's environment, they may have tipped the delicate balances necessary to sustain a small society based on limited resources.

At long last the Van Tilburg *moai*, modern concrete in ancient form, lies on a pile of rubble, its base at the edge of the platform. The NOVA team's final tasks are to raise it to an upright position, crowned with a 1-ton *pukao* in the manner of the ancient Rapanui.

This expedition is not the first to raise a *moai*. In 1955 Thor Heyerdahl and the Norwegian expedition selected a real *moai* lying face down near their camp at Anakena Bay. Twelve Rapanui, supposedly descendants of the Long-Ears, applied the same method to be used by the NOVA team – levers and gradual increments of stones. But they raised the *moai* without using a sledge to protect it. After eighteen days of hard work and virtually undetectable increments, the *moai* stood on its base, gazing with empty eye sockets inland from the bay. The success of the experiment was marred, however, by damage to the statue.

In the 1960s Heyerdahl's colleague William Mulloy returned to try again. Mulloy had the idea that a sledge was necessary to protect the *moai*, and he raised another *moai* attached to a sledge made of parallel beams. But again the statue was badly damaged.

According to Van Tilburg, these previous raisings 'were lifting events that were very, very important and gave us a lot of insight, but they were not in effect real experiments'. Their methods couldn't have been the one used in ancient times, or else we would see the damage in the *moai*, she points out. Moreover, Mulloy's rig 'wasn't really useful in the lifting process', she says.

In her experiment, Van Tilburg promises, 'The rig is going to be a big part of the lifting process, and the statue won't be damaged. It's also going to go a lot quicker.'

The Van Tilburg venture will add one more important variable into the equation as well. No one has yet attempted to raise a *moai* with its *pukao*. No one is sure what the *pukao* represented to their creators. They may have been hats or feathered crowns, or simply hair dressed in a topknot, which Rapanui in real life may have braided, wrapped around their heads and coloured red with clay. A *pukao* could also represent a headdress meant to prepare a warrior for battle. The quarry called Puna Pau, near the main village of Hanga Roa in the western part of the island, was the main source of the red scoria from which the *pukao* were made.

Rapu, the sculptor and descendant of *pukao*-carvers, is in charge of creating a *pukao* for the concrete *moai*. As he picks away at a block of red scoria with a *toki*, Rapu talks through Hito, his interpreter, about the art of *pukao*-carving. He explains that although the scoria is lightweight and therefore easily transported across the island to the *ahu*, it is also a hard rock. The sculptor needs to have a number of *toki* ready, because some will invariably break.

Pukao, he says, were carved by master sculptors who worked exclusively on them. Others would bring them food and water as they worked. Even carving a *pukao* – small compared to an entire *moai* – could take as long as five months, if there wasn't a whole team of sculptors working on it.

'They never worked with the rush of time,' he says. 'It's all based on *mana* and the spirit of time.'

Luckily for the Van Tilburg expedition, the spirit of time has allowed Rapu to deliver his *pukao* on schedule for the raising. Various team members are standing around a secondary stone ramp that has been built for the *pukao*, next to the one atop which the *moai* now lies. Captain Cook wondered how the Rapanui could 'raise such stupendous figures, and afterwards place the large cylindric stones upon their heads'. Some people still think that the *pukao* were attached only after the *moai* was raised, but, as Cristino points out, 'You can imagine the size of the ramp they have to build. I don't see that happening.' Van Tilburg agrees.

They also don't want to attach the *pukao* before raising begins, because that would create a heavier, longer statue and make the early part of the raising much more difficult. The plan is to roll the *pukao* up the small ramp and attach it to the *moai* – and to the wooden frame – when the statue is already partly raised. From that point on, as the entire structure becomes more vertical, gravity will serve to hold the *pukao* against the head with more stability. Cristino hopes that this aspect will make up for the difficulty of raising a suddenly longer figure, with a different centre of gravity.

The workers begin raising the *moai*. They use levers to lift the frame ever so slightly, and fit rocks, recycled from the ramp, underneath for it to rest on. Almost imperceptibly, like the hour hand of a clock, the *moai* begins to stand up. At the end of a day's work, the structure rests on a bed of rocks at an angle of about 30 degrees.

The next step is to attach the *pukao*. The Rapanui men use a pulley to roll the 1-ton red scoria *pukao* up a short, separate ramp. They use a *keke*, the ancient Polynesian tool, to lash it tightly to the *moai*. Then the raising continues, stone by stone. Several of the expert onlookers are taking turns measuring the angle against the horizontal. Soon, however, they begin to squabble over the exact measurement.

'Thirty, exactly thirty,' announces Shiller.

'We've got about 31 degrees and 24 seconds,' insists Jan Van Tilburg.

'We're going to go with 34,' counters Darus Ane.

'The statue or the frame?' Cristino wants to know.

'I go by the frame.'

'No, go by the statue because the angle is different.'

'Thirty-five! It went up five degrees,' shouts Jan Van Tilburg.

'Now it's really moving!' Cristino is pleased. 'The *pukao* is just fitting perfectly in position. Very well done.'

'Well,' says Lee a while later, 'it's about 43 degrees now. You know, mathematically, once it gets beyond 45 degrees, it should get easier rather than more difficult. Getting to here has been the hard part. And as you get nearer and nearer to vertical, and you have less and less weight on the rock pile, that's when it gets quite easy to set the stone upright. But it's hard to control, because you don't have the friction of the load leaning against the rock pile.'

Cristino is confident about the rig's stability. 'By three o'clock, it's going to be very high. By four o'clock it should be up.' He pauses. 'Five o'clock. It's not a promise,' he laughs.

Opposite Pukao *scattered at the exit of the red scoria quarry.*

Erecting the *moai*

SLEDGE

LEVERS

ROCKS

The rock pile grows steadily, but the process becomes more complicated. It is harder and harder for the workmen to find their footing on the rocks and more difficult to control the position of the *moai*. By the time the sun touches the horizon, the pile is 12 feet tall and there is room for only three levers, on which twenty men must jostle for position.

The sun is about to disappear behind the hills, and the *moai* looks like the leaning tower of Rapa Nui, resting against the rock pile at an angle of 55 or 60 degrees from the horizontal. Jan Van Tilburg and some other crew members are leaving tonight for Tahiti, and they dearly want to see the *moai* standing. For them, unlike the ancient Rapanui, the spirit of time is not so leisurely. But today they simply run out of time. A decision is announced: the final raising will wait until morning.

'It's almost dark,' Jo Anne Van Tilburg explains, 'and the rock terrace in front of the *moai* is getting a little precariously balanced. The guys are working hard, maybe pushing a little too hard, and it's a little dangerous at this point.'

Cristino is exhausted. 'It's ten to seven. We worked a good eight hours, and we arrived to a very critical point. We're running out of light, and the *moai* moved a little to the right. We have to be very careful,

LEVERS

SLEDGE

ROCKS

AS THE ANGLE INCREASES, ROCKS FROM THE RAMP ARE USED TO PROP THE *MOAI*. AS THE ROCK PILE GROWS STEEPER, THERE IS ROOM FOR FEWER LEVERERS.

Workers use levering poles to lift the moai *a few inches, then prop it up by placing rocks beneath it.*

because it's at a critical angle, and we could lose the statue. So we have to secure everything tomorrow, put it straight, and control these rocks around it so that people will work safely at the same time.

'It will happen,' he reassures his listeners. 'It's not a problem. That's just a little, little disruption in the general process. If we do that in a couple of hours in the morning, the *moai* will go up by noon.'

The next morning, the men fix their rock scaffolding and recommence the meticulous raising process. As the *moai* moves closer and closer to the point where it can tip right on to the *ahu*, a plethora of tiny adjustments need to be made, first with levers and then with ropes. One such manoeuvre, rotating the statue slightly to align it properly with the platform, particularly pleases Van Tilburg.

'I thought the *moai* was brilliantly adjusted just now,' she comments. 'That base just slid perfectly into position by about, oh, an inch, inch-and-a-half. It was wonderful to stand there and just hear it ssshhh right into position.'

Just at the critical point, when the statue will begin to want to tip on to the platform and measures will have to be taken to control it, the angle controversy flares up again. Shiller and Cristino cannot agree on what angle the *moai* is at or what angle it will be when they're finished.

'No, no, it will never arrive to 90 degrees,' says Cristino.

'The base is going to be horizontal,' Shiller replies. 'What you want to do after that, it's your problem.'

View of the stone pile and partially-raised moai *from behind the* ahu.

Shiller's obsession with getting the perfect angle is getting under Cristino's skin. 'And you say that this is 65 degrees right now,' he says. 'With reference to what?'

'Sixty-five degrees is the angle of the base relative to the horizontal, to the horizon.'

'You mean this angle here?'

'Yes.'

'That's 65?' Cristino is incredulous. 'No way. That's not even 45. I don't know what you're talking about. Sixty-five degrees this way? Come on.'

Shiller seems bemused at Cristino's exasperation, but Cristino has had it after overseeing days of meticulous, stone-by-stone *moai*-raising. He storms away down the path. 'I'm tired of this bullshit!'

A short time later, tempers have cooled, and the *moai*-raising continues. The scientists are too close to success to let minor disagreements get in the way. Cristino and Rapu watch intently as the *moai's* position changes inch by inch, watching for the slightest misalignment.

Van Tilburg, who has had her own flare-ups with Cristino, now expresses nothing but admiration as she describes the final touches he has administered. 'He's placed first sandbags and now sand and small stones underneath the base. That's going to be used to adjust and position the statue into place. It's a sound archaeological and safety move,' she says approvingly.

She and Cristino are watching the final movements together, sharing the satisfaction of watching the long-planned project come to an end. 'In two movements, this will be up,' he says. 'We'll have to go at it very slowly. If we cannot control it, we lose it. This is the most critical point. If we get past this point, the statue will go up without a problem.'

It's five in the afternoon. The *moai* bristles with levers like a defiant porcupine. The workers grunt and heave once more and, like a great ship docking at its pier, the *moai* reaches a stable position on the *ahu*. Is the job finished or not?

'We still have a couple centimetres to go from the vertical,' Cristino estimates.

Below The crew uses ropes to stabilize the moai on its base as it rises higher and higher.

Opposite As the moai approaches a vertical angle, the rock pile grows steeper and narrower and the leverers' footholds more precarious.

'It's your decision,' Van Tilburg defers.

'It's standing perfectly,' he muses. 'The base is flat enough, so I think we don't need to adjust it. We're talking about maybe one degree from the vertical.'

The moment, now that it has arrived, is almost anticlimactic. 'Well done, Claudio,' Van Tilburg beams. 'Brilliantly done, actually. You're to be congratulated.'

Everyone is, and a hearty round of hugs, handshakes, and back-slapping ensues. 'After all this fighting, and all that,' Cristino laughs.

'It took a lot of head butting and arguing and compromise,' Van Tilburg says, shaking her head.

'Anyway,' he says, 'it was quite a creative process. I'm very happy about it.' Even Shiller's angle dispute has been forgotten.

'It's a process that probably they went through in part, in the ancient times,' Van Tilburg notes wryly.

They have little time to savour the victory. A thunderstorm erupts and the driving rain forces everyone to run for shelter. After waiting out the storm, they venture back out to the site. The late afternoon sun angles down on a pacific vision, illuminating a gorgeous double rainbow that rises like a benediction above the brand-new *moai*.

For centuries, the people of Rapa Nui organized themselves into a workforce of substantial power. They managed prodigious projects of sculpture, transport, and construction over the course of years for a single statue. But at some point the network fell apart; the centre would not hold. A society and a spiritual dynasty that must have seemed indomitable fell to pieces in the wake of war and famine. The icons of the passed age were toppled and left to crumble on the ground.

'We made our *moai* of cement with red scoria in it, the soil of the island,' Van Tilburg says of this new icon, the product of her obsession. 'He's as perfect as we can make him, knowing what we know today about shape and form. He has the artistry of the two Rapanui men who worked on him, Cristian and Santi, and he has now the cumulative history of our effort with him. What will happen to him here on the island, I don't know. I don't know whether he'll be accepted and they'll want to keep him or whether they'll want to break him up into a million pieces and throw him in the ocean.'

Opposite *Still attached to the sledge, the* moai *stands upright at last.*

4

ROMAN
BATH

WHAT IS BATHING,
WHEN YOU THINK ABOUT IT?
OIL, SWEAT, FILTH,
GREASY WATER – EVERYTHING LOATHSOME!
Marcus Aurelius

No project was too complex for the engineers of ancient Rome. As their empire spread from Syria to Scotland, the Romans built hundreds of cities and tens of thousands of miles of paved roads. They constructed aqueducts that transported water for hundreds of miles. Among the most remarkable achievements of their civilization were its grand temples, monuments, arenas and libraries.

But of all the achievements of the Roman builders, one stands above the others – the Roman bath. It was the most technologically advanced building of the ancient world. Heat circulated through the walls and floors in a complex system that made some rooms steaming hot, others comfortably warm, and still others refreshingly cool. Piped-in water supplied separate hot and cold pools. Some baths even featured indoor toilets equipped with a primitive flushing system.

Everywhere the Romans went, they built baths. By the reign of Constantine, there were about a thousand baths in the city of Rome alone and many thousands more were scattered throughout the empire. In fact, the Romans built so many of them that the baths served as an architectural laboratory – a place where Roman engineers tried out bold designs and experimented with new materials.

The baths served needs beyond the functional necessities of washing. They were central to the rituals of Roman life. In many parts of the Roman empire, the winters were long and cold. The public bath was a refuge – a place of intoxicating heat where the Romans would spend several hours every day indulging in the elaborate pleasures afforded by their sophisticated heating and plumbing systems: relaxing, soaking, sweating in a steam bath, perhaps having a massage, drinking, gossiping, singing and socializing.

With the fall of the Roman empire, however, customs changed. Perhaps because of the sexual excesses associated with the baths in later years, Christian authorities viewed bathing as indulgent, immoral and decadent. St Benedict warned, 'To those who are well, and especially the young, bathing shall seldom be permitted.' St Francis of Assisi declared dirtiness a sign of a holy man. St Catherine of Sienna never washed. The hygienic secrets of the Roman empire vanished in western Europe, not to reappear for nearly 2000 years.

As the centuries passed, the ancient baths built by the Romans fell into ruins. The furnaces that heated them, being subterranean structures, have largely survived; but many of the buildings that sat above them have crumbled into dust, leaving only questions behind. Without the techniques of modern plumbing and building materials, how did the Romans heat the water to a uniform temperature – and how hot was the water, anyway? How did their heating and ventilation system keep one room constantly hot, a second warm, and a third cold? Without a knowledge of modern physics, how could they predict and control the flow of hot gases through the interior piping of the building?

Previous spread Ruins of the Baths of Caracalla in Rome.

To answer these questions, NOVA assembled a team of archaeologists, historians and engineers in the autumn of 1998 and brought them to the ancient Roman city of Sardis in western Turkey, about 80 kilometres east of the modern

city of Izmir. Their task: to reconstruct an ancient Roman bath using only the tools and technologies available in ancient times. They would have just seven weeks to complete the project. Could they duplicate the achievements of the past?

Columns line the palaestra or outdoor exercise area of the ancient Roman baths at Sardis.

To better appreciate the remarkable accomplishments of the ancient Roman builders, it's useful to journey back to the beginning and trace the fascinating history of bathing and toiletry. It goes back a long way. The first proper toilets we know about are found in the Orkney Islands, off the northern coast of Scotland, and were built about 5000 years ago. They consist of hollowed-out spaces in the walls of crude stone houses, each equipped with a drain that led outside to an underground sewer.

In Mesopotamian Babylon, the ordinary Sumerian defecated into a pot and simply threw the excrement out into the streets. From time to time the authorities would come by and cover the mess with clay. Eventually the layers of clay built up so high that the inhabitants had steps leading down from the streets to their houses. Rich Mesopotamians employed slaves to remove their excrement, but their

houses were equipped with bathing-rooms featuring brick floors and drains: the owners would stand naked while slaves poured water over them. In later centuries they developed indoor toilets of a sort: a hole in the floor with a cesspool under it, over which they would squat to relieve themselves.

Other ancient peoples also had reasonably clean toilet facilities. As far back as 2000 BC the wealthier people of Mohenjo-Daro, in today's Pakistan, had fresh-water toilets connected to open sewer systems, which drained into a large cesspool; they also had public baths. In 1700 BC the Minoans living on the island of Crete had bathtubs, although without drains; they were filled and emptied by hand. At the palace of King Minos at Knossos, the Queen had a flush toilet, the first in history.

The concept of public baths, however, really began to take off with the Greeks. They built public latrines featuring four-hole toilets, sometimes using drains under the streets to carry away the waste. More often, the toilets opened into a pit cleaned out by slaves, who simply threw the excrement into the streets.

By the sixth century BC, Greek cities featured *louteria*, large basins of water placed on pedestals in the open air. After exercising in the *palaestra*, or gymnasium areas, athletes would coat their bodies with sand to soak up the sweat, then splash themselves with water from the *louterion* to wash it off, scraping the last remains with a strigil, a small iron or bronze tool with a curving blade. Sometimes the *louterion* was suspended from a shady olive tree; a slave would tip it to shower water down on to the bather. (Cold water always, to build character; the Greeks believed that hot water might make a man effeminate and soft.) The bather might then wander off to the nearby *exedra*, the philosophical areas, to participate in discussions and arguments or listen to poetry readings.

By the fourth century BC the larger Greek cities had public baths called *balaneia*, supplied with hot water. (Once they had learned how to heat large quantities of water efficiently, the Greeks discovered that bathing in hot water was rather pleasant after all and didn't have the side effects they feared.) Other baths were attached to gymnasia. After exercising, athletes would wash in that lovely hot water and go into a steam room; coming out, they would rinse twice: first in hot water and then in cold.

It was at this time that they worked out an early form of the hypocaust system, the method of heating rooms that the Romans would later adapt and refine. They built a fire in a furnace or open fireplace. Hot gases from the fireplace circulated through a series of channels under a raised floor. The channels were created by the spaces between brick pedestals that supported the floor. On top of the floor the Greeks laid a layer of pumice to keep the bathers' feet from burning. The fire was also used to heat the water for the baths.

The ancient Romans, however, took public bathing much further than the Greeks. For the Greeks, bathing was merely an afterthought to exercise. For the Romans, bathing became the centrepiece of an elaborate social ritual that reflected the complexity – and contradictions – of Roman society.

Unlike the Greeks, who contemplated the beauty and mystery of nature, the Romans focused on the mastery of it. Romans valued the practical, everyday aspects of life. The systems of laws and engineering that provided the twin foundations of their civilization were intended to solve the practical, physical needs of citizen and society.

It should not be forgotten, however, that this vast empire was built on the spoils of war. With ideas, money and an unlimited supply of slave labour appropriated from conquered nations, the Romans secured the means to produce tremendous advances in the machinery of everyday life: roads and harbours, sewers and aqueducts, temples and sports arenas. Life for the people of Rome was to be made as pleasant as possible.

'It's a matter of the social contract that existed between the upper classes of the Roman empire and the lower orders,' explains Garrett Fagan, an assistant professor of classics and ancient Mediterranean studies at Pennsylvania State University and one of the members of the NOVA team. 'The upper classes, who could afford to do so, were expected to provide the lower orders with what the Romans term *commoda* – conveniences, comforts.' This civic responsibility, which the Romans took very seriously, included handouts of money or bread, but also extended to more generous gifts.

In the second century BC the Roman Games were founded to entertain the masses. These games consisted at first of fights between gladiators, a custom that the Romans took over from their Etruscan predecessors. The gladiators were slaves who fought to the death for the pleasure of the crowd. If the victor had put on a good show the audience would give him a 'thumbs-up', and he might be freed. If, though victorious, he was judged to have been too gentle or simply too boring, he got the 'thumbs-down', and was either kept for another contest or killed on the spot.

The scale was continually increased to serve a seemingly insatiable public appetite. When the crowds began to get bored with one man killing another, they began to demand groups of gladiators in immense blood baths. Animals were brought in to claw and devour *venatores*, hired gangs of specially trained hunters; when the hunters began to win too often, the Romans threw in unarmed Christians to be eaten alive by lions for the amusement of the populace.

Supplying animals for the Roman games was a major, highly specialized industry. This Sicilian mosaic depicts hunters capturing and transporting wild beasts.

The baths, however, reflect a more positive aspect of this social contract. Unlike the gladiatorial combats, the idea here was to provide luxury and comfort for the public. It is ironic, then, that the first large public bath was built originally as a private venture by Agrippa.

Marcus Vipsanius Agrippa was born in 63 BC to an unimportant Roman family, but he became friends at school with a young man named Gaius Octavius, later to become the emperor Augustus. Later a general, Agrippa fought under Octavius, and was to command his fleet at the decisive battle of Actium against Mark Antony.

With Octavius (now Augustus) the undisputed ruler of Rome, Agrippa returned a rich man. He spent six years building a magnificent bath for public use, and by 19 BC it was finished. Situated in a landscaped park with an artificial river and a lake for swimming, it had a vast rotunda 25 metres in diameter, surrounded by other rooms. Fresh water was brought in by aqueduct; the baths were heated by hypocausts under the floors and channels through which the hot air flowed inside the walls. There was an exercise yard, a *palaestra*, so that bathers could build up a sweat before taking the waters.

Upon his death Agrippa asked that the bath remain available for the free use of the Roman people – parks, gardens and all. It was followed by the even more splendid baths of Nero, Trajan, Caracalla and Diocletian. Each successive emperor strove to outdo his predecessors in the display of wealth, opulence and, implicitly, political power. The marbles that panelled the walls and floors, for instance, were drawn from the far reaches of the empire – Egypt, Turkey, Greece, northern Italy – as many as ten different kinds of marble from fifteen different countries.

'The symbolic power of this decorative magnificence,' says Fagan, 'not only represents the economic power of the emperor but the reach of Rome, which extends across the Mediterranean and can bring all this to Rome for the pleasure of the everyday citizen.' By providing a sense of luxury, he adds, the emperor could assure citizens that they share in the empire's wealth and remind them of the privileges they enjoy as Roman citizens.

Nero's bath, built in AD 60, spread out over 3000 square metres. Caracalla's bath, built in AD 217, covered an incredible 140,000 square metres – about 27 acres. The decorations in the bathing rooms were awe-inspiring, with marbles, mosaics, frescos, gilded bronze elements, and towering columns 50 feet high, weighing over 90 tons. The grounds also included parks and, probably, libraries, and certainly lecture halls. Later innovations included open-air pools, sports and games rooms, bars, and theatres for plays, poetry readings, debates and concerts.

Men and women bathed together, most likely naked and at best quite scantily covered. Although it's hard to generalize about practices that may have varied from place to place and from time to time, it's clear that sexual activity, both hetero- and homosexual, was strongly associated with the baths. The Roman epigrammatist Marcus Valerius Martialis, known as Martial, writing in the first century AD, tells of one Roman whose 'line of vision keeps below waist level; he devours with his eyes the boys under the showers'. Whether sexual activities took place in the baths themselves, either publicly or privately, or whether interested parties simply met there to make other arrangements, is uncertain.

When the Emperor Diocletian came to power, he sought to accomplish the unthinkable – to build a public bath even more glorious than the Baths of Caracalla. Opened at the turn of the fourth century, the Baths of Diocletian covered almost 30 acres, large enough to allow more than 10,000 people to mingle at once. Everything inside was bigger, taller and more opulent than any bath that had come before it. Contemporary sources praise the beauty of the baths – the multicoloured marbles, the light streaming in the windows, and the water trickling from elaborately sculpted bronze spouts.

'It's clear that the Romans enjoyed their baths tremendously,' Fagan says. 'To step into the bath house was to step into the arms of pleasure… an altogether joyful experience.'

Not all baths were on the scale of these grand imperial baths, of course. Far more common was the smaller local bath, more on the scale of the neighbourhood pub, where fifty or sixty neighbours could meet each afternoon and socialize. And finally, there were the private baths. Only the wealthiest Roman citizens could afford to build a private bath for the pleasure of family and intimate friends.

By the second century AD Rome boasted eleven imperial baths and more than 800 neighbourhood baths, all to serve the needs of a city of about a million people. For people in all walks of life, the two- or three-hour bath, usually in the afternoon before dinner, was the highpoint of the day. For those enjoying the full experience of an afternoon at the imperial baths, the ritual went something like this:

You would take off your clothes and leave them in a niche in the wall of the *apodyterium*, where they'd be guarded by a slave. Locks were rarely used, and thieves were everywhere – you couldn't leave your things unguarded. (In fact, archaeologists have found small scrolls of lead inscribed with curses in the ruins at Bath, England. If someone stole your clothes, you would scratch a curse in the metal – 'May your hair fall out and may you never have sex again!' – and throw it into the bath, hoping the gods would avenge a crime for which you had no civic recourse.)

After changing in the *apodyterium*, you would saunter into the warm-air *tepidarium*, where you could relax while a slave applied oils and perhaps sand to your body. You might then go outside to wrestle a bit and work up a light sweat for what followed. A slave might wipe your skin with a strigil (remember, there was no soap in ancient Rome) or a sponge. This is a good time to hire a depilator, or hair-plucker, to remove body hair, which was considered unsightly to the Romans of ancient days.

In the more elaborate baths, you could go on to the dry-air heated *laconicum*, with water thrown on to heated stones to make the air breathable, or to the *sudatorium*, a more humid but still gently heated room. There you would relax while the heat seeped into your bones. After a while you would move to the *caldarium* for real heat, with cooling water available for sprinkling from a vat (*labrum*). Then on to an alcove with a pool big enough for a dozen men and women at a time; there you would sit on the steps to the pool and socialize for hours. At the top of any single man's agenda was wangling an invitation for dinner that evening, preferably from someone who could advance his career.

Finally you would rinse off the remaining oils with fresh water, and pop into the *frigidarium* for a character-building swim in an icy pool. Before leaving you could, if you liked, get a massage in the *unctorium*. Such were the simple pleasures of the baths of Caracalla and Diocletian.

A bather might also want to take advantage of the toilet facilities. A typical bath featured a line of toilets situated next to each other in what today would seem uncomfortably close surroundings, leaving no room for privacy or prestige. The Romans had no toilet paper; instead, they used a long stick with a sponge on one

The closely spaced seats of this ruined Roman latrine show how little privacy they offered. The plank on which users sat is placed above a pit cleaned by slaves.

end to wipe themselves. When finished, the user would rinse the sponge end in a pot of water; the apparatus was then passed from one person to the other along the line of toilets.

While most contemporary accounts of Roman baths, particularly the grand imperial baths, describe their beauty, luxury and comfort, the baths might be viewed somewhat differently by an observer from the twenty-first century, for the Romans knew very little about hygiene. Garrett Fagan notes that physicians would prescribe public bathing as a remedy for all kinds of illnesses – skin diseases, bowel problems, urinary infections, fevers. It was common to find scum floating on the surface of the pools. Instead of throwing it away, the Romans would collect it along with the globs of oil and sand that splattered from the slaves' strigils and mix it into an ointment called *gloios*, which was used to make an unguent for relieving headaches. The Romans remained blissfully ignorant of the existence of microbes and germs and attributed any ill effects of bathing to the intervention of the gods.

Although wealthy patricians did attend, the baths were crowded with the common people of Rome. Seneca the Younger, who lived close to a public bath, complained about them in his *Moral Epistles*:

> I'm surrounded by the most terrible racket, my lodgings are right by the baths... When the top gymnasts are training and swinging their lead dumbbells, when they are labouring or at any rate pretending to labour, I hear them groan; when they exhale I hear whistling and rasping breath. And if I get some bather who wants no more than a cheap massage, then I hear the sound of the hand slapping the shoulders – a different sound depending if it lands curved or flat. But if a ballplayer arrives and starts keeping score, I am really done for. And let us not leave out the picker of quarrels, the petty thief caught in the act, the man who is in love with the sound of his own voice in the bath. Nor should we forget the swimming pool and the mighty crash of water every time someone dives in... and then imagine the hair-plucker who keeps up a perpetual falsetto yapping to attract attention, only silent when he's setting someone's armpits on fire and making the other person cry out in his stead. Then there's the man selling drinks with singsong cries, the sausage seller, the confectioner and all those cookshop boys, each with his own characteristic inflection to cry his wares...

In the baths, people of every stripe spent many hours playing games, cleaning themselves, or simply relaxing in a congenial and stimulating atmosphere. Even slaves were allowed to take part in the pleasures of the baths, although they may not have had as much free time to enjoy them. This is especially surprising given the rigid stratification of Roman society. In the world outside the baths, distinctions of status were strictly enforced. The clothing of each social class was strictly regulated. A special law once required prostitutes to bleach their hair so they could be distinguished from more respectable ladies.

The nudity of the baths may have meant that one couldn't easily tell one's inferiors from one's peers. Some experts argue that the baths represented a hole in the ozone layer of the social hierarchy. But the truth may be more complex. Even when naked, Fagan points out, there were many subtle ways for privileged Romans to assert their rank. Like any public venue, bathing provided an opportunity for the rich to flaunt their wealth. The Roman baths may have promoted a sense of community, but they may also have served to reinforce the community's rules.

The purpose of the NOVA experiment is both to build an authentic Roman bath and to experience some of its pleasures. Given the time, technology and resources available, the NOVA team decides to reconstruct a small, private bath – the type of bath a wealthy Roman citizen might have built beside or near his home.

The venture is more complicated than it seems. The most obvious question is what, exactly, constitutes a Roman bath? The Romans took their civilization to every country they conquered. Although one of the hallmarks of that civilization was standardization – essential to the efficient administration of an empire – there was nonetheless significant variation in the design and engineering of Roman baths at different times or in different places.

For example, how did the Romans heat their baths? Did the hot air rise through hollow walls and vent directly out, or were the interior walls connected to one or to several flues? Did these systems vary in different times and places, or sometimes combine in one building?

This is no small detail, for without electric motors to pump the heat about and direct it where it was wanted, the Romans had to rely on flues to harness the natural movements of heated gases. They had, of course, no knowledge of modern physics to guide them, and with the intricacies of gas pressures and temperatures varying as a function of distance from the primary furnace, as well as with the thickness and materials of the walls, the problem gets very complex. And if the NOVA team gets just one aspect of it wrong, the draughts won't draw properly, the hot gases won't circulate as planned, the building won't heat, and the experiment will fail.

Another problem is that no one knows precisely how hot the water was. There are anecdotal descriptions of people fainting after a few minutes in the hot bath. On the other hand, the Romans went there to enjoy themselves, not to suffer. So the baths must have been only pleasantly warm – perhaps about 40 degrees Centigrade (100 degrees Fahrenheit). In hot air we sweat, and the evaporation of the sweat cools the skin. Of course, in a hot bath that mechanism doesn't work. Lounging in water of 100 degrees F, approximately the same temperature as our bodies, we are comfortably warm. But as the bath water gets hotter, heat flows from the water into our bodies, which must then get rid of the excess heat – and we have no normal physiological mechanism for doing so. The result is severe discomfort that can become dangerous.

Like the temperature of the water, the air temperature in the various rooms is

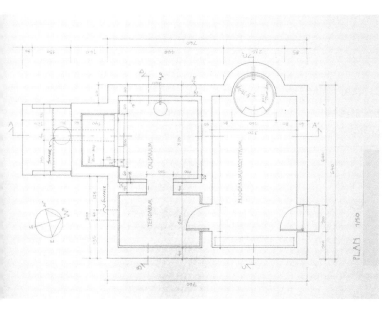

unknown. In addition, no one knows if the hot gases flowing through the walls were intended to provide heat to the rooms, or if they served merely as insulation to keep the rooms from cooling off, with all the heat being provided from the hypocausts below.

The answers to most of these questions are based on speculation. The Romans left no blueprints, no technical specifications of any of the baths they built. All archaeologists have to go on are the ruins that are left and occasional descriptions written thousands of years ago. The best known is a brief treatise by the Roman architect Vitruvius in the first century BC, laying out some of the specifications for building a bath. However, it gives only a very general description; key information, particularly about the plumbing, heating and venting systems, is missing.

Modern physics and engineering can also contribute to an understanding of the kinds of solutions that may have worked in the past. The NOVA team brings these various forms of expertise to bear as its members seek the best way to find answers: by building a bath themselves.

The team is led by Fikret Yegül, a professor in the department of the history of art and architecture at the University of California at Santa Barbara. A leading scholar in the field of architectural history, he grew up in Turkey and has spent almost thirty summers working with the internationally staffed and financed Sardis Archaeological Expedition, painstakingly reconstructing the sites in that ancient city, including the baths and gymnasium.

After a lifetime of studying Roman baths, Yegül is ready to turn theory into practice. He has created a detailed blueprint for the kind of Roman bath that would have been built in ancient Asia Minor. His design, refined with the help of Turkish engineer Teoman Yalçinkaya, another member of the Sardis Archaeological Expedition, will serve as the basis for the NOVA project; Yalçinkaya will lead the construction.

The building will consist of three main rooms: a *tepidarium* for changing clothes, a *caldarium* equipped with a hot bath, and a *frigidarium* featuring a cold pool. It will be topped with vaulted roofs and boast a state-of-the-art Roman heating and ventilation system.

The NOVA team members meet for the first time in Bath, England, in September 1998 to review and discuss the blueprints. (Aptly, Bath is the site of one of the last grand Roman baths ever built.) Joining Yegül and Yalçinkaya are archaeologist Tony Rook and his associate Bryan Scott. Rook is a former building materials specialist, who discovered the ruins of a Roman bath in his home town of Welwyn, England, almost thirty years ago. Today it is a museum visited by hundreds of schoolchildren every year. Rook and Scott, an architectural technician, hope some day to reconstruct a working replica of that bath and see this as an opportunity to learn how. Like the others, they bring both passions and prejudices to the project and it is not long before conflicting perspectives begin to surface.

As Rook and Scott look over Yegül's blueprints, they begin to raise questions about the layout. 'Looking at this from the point of view of the sort of ruins that we have in Britain rather than in the eastern Mediterranean, there are various things which worry us,' Rook says. For instance, in most domestic Roman baths Rook has studied, the cold basin in the *caldarium* – a kind of sink – is housed in an apse. This feature is missing in Yegül's design.

The difference may simply be a regional one. 'That kind of thing is less

The caldarium *in the Roman baths complex at Pompeii featured a grooved roof, so that moisture could drip down the walls. Note the cold basin placed in the apse.*

common, extremely rare, in eastern baths,' Yegül assures him.

But Rook has more important worries. 'It's not common practice, in my knowledge, to have the *tepidarium* and *caldarium* different sizes,' he persists.

Yegül admits this is less common, but defends the decision to make the *caldarium* larger. 'It was very conscious, although we may disagree there,' he notes. 'The *caldarium* is the culminating space of the Roman bath, a unique and important space. People will spend the greatest time there, gossiping and talking and even eating and drinking. So I wanted to create a modicum of grandiosity – if you can call a ten-foot by ten-foot space grandiose.'

The most challenging – and controversial – aspect of the design, however, is the heating and venting system. According to Yegül's plan, the building will be heated by a furnace. Gases from the furnace will flow under the floors of the *tepidarium* and *caldarium*, and then will be channelled upwards through *tubuli* in the walls. (*Tubuli* are hollow bricks. When the bricks are arranged in vertical stacks, gases can flow upwards through the hollow space at the centre. The *tubuli* also have holes cut in their sides. When the bricks are placed side by side, these holes create horizontal channels that allow the gases to flow across the walls.) The *tubuli* will be placed in three walls of the *caldarium* and one wall of the *tepidarium*. Since there are no *tubuli* in the three remaining walls of the *tepidarium*, it will be heated only through the floor, making it just moderately warm compared to the *caldarium*. There will be no heating at all in the *frigidarium*, as its name suggests.

But for the heating system to work, the gases from the furnace must be drawn upwards and ultimately vented out into the open air. One of the key questions facing the NOVA team is how the Romans vented their baths. There are many ruins in which the walls remain standing, so the *tubuli* can be seen clearly. But the roofs of most baths have collapsed; all in all, there is very little archaeological evidence to draw on.

The task of evaluating the reliability of the system will fall to Max Fordham, an engineer who has designed some of the most complex interior climate-control systems in the world, including Britain's Tate Gallery and Savoy Theatre. He also teaches at the University of Bath. His role on the NOVA team is to bring modern engineering expertise to bear in evaluating the design.

According to Yegül's initial plan, gases would be drawn from the furnace in several directions. Some would be channelled under the floors to flues running from the hypocaust to the roof. Others were supposed to flow upward through the *tubuli* in the walls. The *tubuli* were blocked at the top, so that the hot gases would be forced to diffuse through the horizontal channels between the bricks. As the gases cooled, they would seep downwards towards the hot floor and, as they gained heat, rise again.

Before the meeting in Bath, Yegül had circulated this plan to the other team members. Fordham had questioned whether there would be enough of a draught to draw the gases through the walls if the *tubuli* were blocked at the top. The system, he said, would heat the floor but not the walls. He proposed leaving some

of the *tubuli* open at the top and installing a dropped ceiling below the arched roof, in effect creating a double ceiling. According to this plan, the gases could flow through the hypocaust, up the *tubuli*, into the space between the two ceilings, and out through one or more flues. Although the solution might have worked well from an engineering point of view, the archaeological evidence did not support it and the idea was dismissed as non-Roman.

By the time the group meets in Bath, Yegül has developed a different plan. In this version, some of the *tubuli* are left open at the top. Gases that flow upward out of the *tubuli* will gather in a collecting channel that runs along the top of the wall. The collecting channel in turn vents to the flues, joining the gases that flow directly to the flues through the hypocaust below. Gases from the blocked-off *tubuli* will circulate in the walls until they are drawn out through one of the open *tubuli*.

Rook and Scott like the collecting channel, but question the authenticity of the venting plan. They argue that all of the *tubuli* should be open at the top, and that the collecting channel should vent directly to the outside. They point to the existence of what may have been ventilation holes in the baths at Herculaneum to support their point.

A key question is whether the *tubuli* played a role in heating the walls or

Tubuli *from the ruins of a Roman bath.*

Hot gases circulate among the pilae *beneath the floor of the* caldarium, *then circulate through holes between the* tubuli *set in the walls. When the gases reach the top of the* tubuli *they gather in a collecting channel and are vented through a slender chimney to the air outside.*

simply acted as insulators. If the *tubuli* vent upward, they will help to heat the room by channelling hot gases through the walls; if they are blocked off, they simply help to retain the heat by keeping the gases circulating through the walls. In the latter case, the baths would be heated entirely through the floor. Rook and Scott argue that both the walls and the floor should radiate heat. 'That's what creates the experience of the Roman bath,' Scott emphasizes.

What Yegül has designed, however, is a mixed system, in which some of the *tubuli* act as heaters and others as insulators. 'A few of our *tubuli* will be actively connected to the heating system, and they will be part of the draught,' he explains. 'And the others, we're hoping, will just be inert blankets, not radiating heat but helping to retain the heat in the room.' In this way, he says, the space will be heated by both walls and floor. Drawing on his experience with baths in other regions of the Roman empire, he finds ample archaeological evidence for this kind of design.

'This appears to be one area where there is a significant difference between the eastern and the western empires,' Scott concedes. 'I certainly wouldn't question your experience and your research in this, Fikret.'

Back in his laboratory, Fordham has used computational fluid dynamics (CFD) to analyse the flow of gases in Yegül's revised design. 'This is a pretty difficult circulation pattern to envisage,' Fordham reports, reviewing the blueprint. 'I'm slightly sceptical about it.' He concludes that the system is still likely to be more effective at heating the floor of the baths than the walls.

Rook wants to get back to the authenticity issue. 'I think we're in considerable danger here of getting lost in the fact that we have modern physics,' he says. 'What we're trying to do here is to construct something the Romans would have built, not something –'

'But I don't think the Romans would habitually have built something that didn't work,' Fordham interrupts. 'They might have made mistakes occasionally, but not as a habit.' Whether or not the Romans understood the physics underlying the flow of hot gases, he argues, they must have experimented with different designs until they found one that worked. Thus modern physics can help to predict (even if retroactively) what solutions they are most likely to have chosen.

Rook is not happy with this way of approaching things. 'What's the Latin for CFD?' he asks pointedly. 'We've gone a long, long way from the Romans here.'

'One of the things about modern technology and engineering and buildings,' Fordham responds patiently, 'is that by applying the most modern, sophisticated physics you're able to show how things worked that everyone before thought *couldn't* have worked.' Despite his reservations, he is willing to give Yegül's plan a try. 'I'm very interested in trying to see how this works. Never mind whether we predict whether it works or not.'

This last comment gets a rise out of Yegül: 'Don't think that this is something that we have drawn up *thinking* that it would work. This is something for which we have plenty of models.'

'But what we know,' Fordham persists, 'is that they made it. We don't know whether they worked.'

'They made hundreds of them,' Yegül answers. 'They must have worked.'

'Yes,' says Fordham, 'but they would have heated the *floor*. All you have to do to get a really hot room is heat the floor really hot. Whether the system will work the way Yegül wants it to is a different question. I get very impatient,' he adds, 'with people who design things on hunches and won't take engineering calculations into the process of design.'

'But this is not a design we created!' Yegül exclaims. 'We can't even take much credit for creativity here. This is really a duplication. It is an imitation of a type of Roman bath that I have seen and worked again and again.'

The ruins of the Aqua Claudia, built to transport water to Rome, are testimony to the ingenuity of the ancient Roman engineers.

With that last word, the NOVA team agrees to give Yegül's plan a try. They will travel to Sardis the following month to begin construction.

The question of water supply is one problem the group will not deal with. To reconstruct a Roman aqueduct would be far beyond the NOVA team's capabilities: these tremendous feats of engineering would be marvels in any age. The first Roman aqueduct was built in 312 BC; until that time Rome had depended on its wells and springs for water, but in that year Appius Claudius realized that the population had swollen to such a degree that there wasn't enough fresh water for them, and he built an underground aqueduct 7 miles in length.

In 144 BC the city's population had once again outgrown its water supply, and the Aqua Marcia was built, bringing water from springs in the Sabine hills through a channel 60 miles long. Two hundred years later, the Aqua Claudia was built to draw water from the same region. Crossing the low plains between the hills and Rome, the two aqueducts were supported on a series of arches that still stand in places today.

Peter Aicher, another contributor to the NOVA project and a professor of classics at the University of Southern Maine, describes the system: 'Rome ended up with a million people, and needed lots of water. And they got it through eleven aqueducts spanning over 300 miles of channels. We don't know for sure, but we figure there were 150 to 200 gallons per person, per day, which I think compares favourably with modern cities. Once Rome fell, nothing comparable was found again until the nineteenth century. By any standards, that's a lot of water for the city.' In fact, average water use in the United States is about 185 gallons per person per day. Thus the system of aqueducts the Romans built provided ampler and cleaner supplies of fresh water than most people on Earth enjoy today.

The Romans were not the first people to build aqueducts to transport water. The ancient Assyrians tapped underground aquifers in hills and brought the water to their cities in long canals. Sargon II probably brought this technique back from Turkey and Iran, along with the booty from his wars there. Large dams and associated canals supplied ancient Nineveh with water, crossing valleys and going through hills on the way. The Greeks too had built numerous aqueducts before the Romans took them over. Herodotus describes an aqueduct more than half a mile long that was built in 530 BC to supply Samos, and by the second century BC Pergamum had a subterranean aqueduct 25 miles long.

The first problem in building an aqueduct is finding a source of fresh water. Sometimes this is a simple task, as when a region has abundant natural lakes or springs, but most of the Earth's fresh-water supplies are hidden underground, and searching them out is a difficult science – perhaps even an art. When Agrippa built an aqueduct to service his bath, his military engineers were at a loss to find a source of water until a local girl pointed out to them a subterranean spring. The

The Trevi Fountain in Rome, depicting the discovery of the springs that supplied the Aqua Virgo.

channel was named the Aqua Virgo in her honour. Rome's famous Trevi Fountain, which is still fed from the same spring, celebrates her feat with a relief sculpture showing the girl pointing out the spring as the engineers gape in astonishment.

The aqueduct's source must be located higher than its ultimate destination, since the Romans, with no pumps capable of lifting the water efficiently during its journey, had to rely on gravity, following a long, gradual slope from the mountains to the city. The course of the aqueduct had to be planned carefully, avoiding any steep upward slopes. Even a steep downward slope would be dangerous, since over time the fast-running water would erode the walls. Laying out the course was a monumental task, but the Romans did this routinely.

Next came the problem of water purity. They solved this by building settling

tanks in which the water collected while sand and silt settled to the bottom, and by exposing the water to the oxygen of the atmosphere as it cascaded along the aqueduct. There is no evidence that the Romans knew of the necessity for keeping water oxygenated; it is probably just a lucky break that their system provided for it.

After leaving the settling tanks, 80 per cent of a typical Roman aqueduct ran underground in tunnels. At first glance these would seem more difficult to build than above-ground structures, but such tunnels actually require less material than archways and last longer, since they are less susceptible to erosion and earthquakes. Where they had to travel over valleys or low-lying plains, great arched bridges were built to avoid long detours or a loss in elevation.

Finally, the water reached Rome. Near today's Porta Maggiore, one of the highest spots in the city, eight aqueducts converged on the city. At this point the system changed from a gravity-driven one to a network of closed, pressurized pipes that carried the water to houses, fountains, industries and, of course, the baths throughout the city. Most of the pipes were made of lead – hence the word 'plumbing' from the Latin word for lead: *plumbum*.

Meanwhile, the NOVA team has arrived in Turkey to begin construction on the first Roman bath to be built in more than 1500 years. To supply the bath they will build a small reservoir that draws from a simple portable tank instead of an aqueduct. This is actually not much of a cheat, since in Roman times many homes with similar private baths would use rainwater collected in barrels rather than connecting to a piped water supply.

NOVA decided to build the bath near the tiny village of Sart, the site of the ancient city of Sardis. This is an area rich in ancient history. In the sixth century BC Sardis was ruled by Croesus, the Lydian king of fabled wealth. Conquered next by Cyrus the Great of Persia, Sardis continued to flourish under Hellenistic, Roman and Byzantine rule until it was conquered by the Turks and deserted.

The valley in which it was situated is still lush and fertile, however. NOVA's bath will be built on the edge of an olive grove near a road lined with pomegranate trees. Each day, flocks of sheep pass by on their way to grazing land at a higher elevation. Across the nearby Pactolus River, the columns of the Roman Temple of Artemis rise above the hills. And not far away stands the imposing reconstructed façade of the Imperial Bath Gymnasium built by the Romans in the first century AD.

Yalçinkaya and Yegül arrive early to prepare the site. The *caldarium* will face south to take advantage of solar heating – 'the ideal Roman way of doing things', as Yegül says. Once they have marked out the foundation, Yegül departs for home in California, leaving the construction under Yalçinkaya's supervision. He has only two weeks to lay the foundation and build the walls. Then the rest of the team will reassemble to oversee construction of the heating and plumbing system.

NOVA team member Garrett Fagan takes advantage of this hiatus to experience a Turkish *hamam* – a direct descendant of a Roman bath. In the centre of the bustling city of Izmir, Garrett finds a *hamam* that has been serving customers for more than 300 years. And although the process has changed a bit over the centuries, Fagan discovers the similarities are striking.

The room he enters is hot, over 100 degrees Fahrenheit. For ten minutes he lies on a large marble slab that accommodates half a dozen bathers. The slab and the room are heated by an underfloor heating system not unlike an ancient Roman hypocaust. Once he is completely bathed in perspiration, an attendant begins to give him a dry massage – an optional element for a Roman bather but a fixture of

Frontal view of the restored baths/gymnasium at Sardis.

Mosaic from the baths at Sardis.

the Turkish experience. The attendant then uses an abrasive glove called a *kesa* to rub him down and scrub the dirt from his skin. After about twenty minutes, he is given a slow, gentle soaping and then rinsed off in cold water. There are no women inside – men and women bathe separately either in a different *hamam* or at different times. Unlike the Roman bath which lasted several hours, the entire experience takes about half an hour.

Back at the site, the work is moving along smoothly. Yalçinkaya has hired Ibrahim Akyar as foreman. Akyar, in turn, has hired about a dozen men from the village to serve as the construction crew. Most of the men are local farmers who tend olive groves, grow grapes for raisins or raise small flocks of sheep. But in the summers many of them work as labourers for the Sardis Archaeological Expedition. Each year, the academics who comprise the Sardis expedition team descend on this small village to continue the painstaking work of excavating the ancient Lydian, Roman and Byzantine ruins that abound in this area. Akyar and some of the older members of the NOVA construction crew did the hard work of restoring the façade of the Imperial Bath Gymnasium at Sardis – placing each brick and stone under the direction of the archaeologists.

The crew is working every day to keep construction of the NOVA bath on schedule, even Saturday and Sunday. The only time they take off from the work is Friday afternoon – the Muslim Sabbath. Around noon they go home to change

their clothes and then to the village mosque to pray. They'll return to the site around three in the afternoon and continue working until dusk.

And their hard work pays off. At the end of two weeks, the foundation is laid and the stone and brick walls are complete. From the outside, it's beginning to look like a real Roman bath. Fikret Yegül arrives first – just in time to see the walls that surround the furnace take shape. He stops the masonry work for just a moment and places a 5000 Turkish lira coin (worth about a penny) in the mortar. It's common to find a Roman coin embedded in a building wall and Fikret wants to continue the tradition. He also wants to ensure that 2000 years from now, archaeologists will know when this building was constructed.

The simplicity of the bath's exterior belies the technological complexity that challenged Roman builders 2000 years ago. But even its exterior construction demonstrates two of the Romans' greatest contributions to architectural design and construction: the domed roof and the material known as concrete.

Like most of Rome's contributions, the use of concrete was more a matter of improvement than a completely original discovery. Various forms of the mixture have been found in structures dating as far back as ancient Egypt. In fact, concrete is really a clever idea added to cement, and cement goes all the way back to the Stone Age, when early humans used fire to create lime. They must have observed that when limestone, a common rock composed of calcium carbonate, fell into a fire, it miraculously changed form. Today, a chemist would explain that when carbon dioxide (CO_2) is released from calcium carbonate ($CaCO_3$) it leaves lime (CaO). If that chunk of lime then happened to fall into water, these early observers would have seen another change taking place: as the CaO absorbs water, it becomes a gooey mass which later hardens or 'sets'. Since those early discoveries, virtually every civilization on earth has used wet lime to cement stones together.

Rook speculates about the further evolution of concrete: 'This stuff's absolutely marvellous for going between stones. Somebody must have said, "Well, if we're going to put it between stones, why don't we just add some stones directly into it?"' Once they mixed in sand and rock, they found that the new material – concrete – could make a wall as strong as one made of stone and mortar.

The Romans then added a new ingredient to the recipe. 'If you happened to be in Naples,' Rook points out, 'there was no sand, but there was lots and lots of volcanic ash.' The great advantage of mixing volcanic ash into concrete, he explains, is that it makes concrete waterproof. 'If you pour water over it, it just absorbs more moisture and becomes even harder, so you can use it for pilings to hold up a bridge, to line aqueducts, or for the bottoms of baths and things like that.' In regions where there was no volcanic ash, Romans used broken tile instead, which worked almost as well.

Because concrete can be cast into different shapes, you can build almost anything with it. The Pantheon is made almost entirely of concrete; the huge baths of Caracalla and Diocletian could not have been built without it. In Asia Minor, baths were commonly built of stone, brick and mortar – the materials the NOVA team is using – but concrete was used in places. The NOVA team will use it to cover the arched brick roof.

Tony Rook demonstrates how to make concrete.

The domed or vaulted roof was one of Rome's greatest architectural advances. The concept goes back to the realization that it is possible to bridge a large space by leaning two small stones together across it, a discovery that goes all the way back to the Neolithic age. Indeed, triangular arches pre-dating those of the Romans are to be found throughout the Mediterranean, including some in ancient Greece.

The domed roof of the Pantheon was the culmination of a technology honed by the building of thousands of Roman baths.

The great step forward over these was the introduction of the curved arch, but this too occurred before Roman times; it is seen in the Tigris–Euphrates Valley as early as 4000 BC. It was used in Egypt and Assyria, but became most common in Italy, under the Etruscan progenitors of the Romans, who recognized its value and adopted it as the major architectural feature in the design of their buildings. In this kind of arch, the weight of the centre stone creates a horizontal force pushing the lower stones of the arch away from the centre. In a well-designed arch, this force holds the structure together by counteracting the force of gravity, which would otherwise pull the angled stones inward. If the weight of the supports is not great enough, however, the stones will buckle outwards under pressure from above and the whole thing will collapse.

The necessary supporting force is not easy to calculate and in ancient times there was simply no way to do it, so an architect had to guess whether his arch would support itself or collapse. This is no way to establish an architectural career, so pre-Roman civilizations used the arch only in places where the horizontal retaining force would obviously be sufficient: for example, in openings in mountain walls or underground in tombs.

The main Roman innovation in the use of the arch was to free it for use anywhere. It was the Romans who learned how to estimate the necessary support weight and so to use the arch to enclose open spaces wherever they wanted.

Today this is no problem, and the vaulted roof over the NOVA bath is put into place. First, the workers build a series of wooden arch forms and array them in two parallel rows on the roof. They nail wooden planks across each row of arch forms until two perfect arches take shape. Then using the planking as a guide, they begin laying alternating courses of bricks and mortar. Finally they spread a layer of concrete on top.

It takes several days for the roof to dry. The construction has fallen a little behind schedule, and Yalçinkaya decides to take down the planking that has supported the roof a little early so that the team can begin work on the heating system. Tearing down the planking is a harrowing process. If the roof isn't dry enough, or if its design or construction is flawed in any way, it could cave in. But as the planks peel off safely, one by one, the workers breathe a sigh of relief and move on to the next challenge.

By the time the team members reassemble, the building looks just like a real Roman bath – except that the inside is empty. Now comes the toughest challenge: building the heating system. Rook, Scott and Fordham find Yegül and Yalçinkaya

A worker puts in place the wooden frames to support the arched roof of the NOVA bath; planking on the other vault is already in place. Layers of brick and concrete will be laid over the planking; when all is dry, the wooden frames and planking will be removed.

in the *caldarium* marking the layout for the *pilae*, pillars made of brick tiles and mortar that will support the raised floor. Nearby is a stack of *bipedalis*, the broad, flat tiles that will be placed on top of the *pilae* to form the flooring.

'Good Lord!' Rook exclaims, laughing, as he gets his first look at them. 'These don't look very much like the tiles we were talking about, do they? What happened?'

Piled up on the left are roofing tiles, on the right bricks for making chimneys and in the background tubuli *for lining the walls.*

The tiles had been problematic from the beginning. When Yegül began to design the bath, Yalçinkaya discovered, in consultation with the owner of a local brick factory, that it would take much too long to make the clay tiles to a standard Roman design (about 60 cm by 60 cm, according to the architect Vitruvius's treatise). So he and Yegül proposed making the *bipedalis* a bit smaller, hoping that they would dry more quickly.

At the meeting in Bath, however, Scott suggested a different solution: instead of making the tiles smaller, why not make them out of concrete? After all, if *bipedalis* throughout the Roman empire were the same size, there must be a reason for it. Switching to a smaller tile size would also cause changes in the design of the hypocaust system: the *pilae* would have to be placed closer together, and it's not clear if this will allow for the proper circulation of gases under the floor. Yegül, however, pointed out that there is archaeological evidence of at least a few baths in which the *pilae* are placed more closely. After some discussion, Scott's suggestion was defeated, not only on the grounds of authenticity but because the change in material might affect the functioning of the heating system as well.

Now Yalçinkaya, who is responsible for all details large and small, explains the latest developments. 'We had problems with the manufacture of the tiles,' he says. They were being made by a local brick factory. Even at a reduced size, they were still so big and thick that they didn't dry properly and began to crack even before they were fired.

Yalçinkaya consulted a famous ceramic artist in Izmir. His advice, as it turned out, was to make the tiles the way the Romans did – by hand. And so, in the corner of a modern brick factory, the clay was mixed manually. Ash and straw were added in to aid in the drying and special wooden moulds were built.

'But then these tiles began to split during the air-drying process, just before going into the kiln,' Yalçinkaya tells Rook. 'So then we consulted again, with several different people who know about clay. I mean, if it is cement, we know exactly what to do. But with soil it is different. The behaviour of soil is very different than anything else.'

Scott chimes in: 'More unpredictable.'

'Yes,' Yalçinkaya agrees. The manufacturers tried twice again, he continues, making holes in the tiles and rotating them every day during the drying process. 'But at the end, we saw that at this time of the year there is not enough–'

Rook: 'Humidity?'

'No. The humidity is all right,' says Yalçinkaya. 'But it was too hot some days, and it was colder the next day.' The variation in the daily temperature and the lack of time, the men agree, doomed their efforts.

'I tell you, these Romans were clever people,' says Rook. 'They knew how to do it and we don't.'

'But the Romans had more time!' protests Scott. 'That's the point, isn't it? The Romans had a good deal longer to actually make the tiles and weather them and allow the drying process to take place.' Because the baths were often built to a uniform standard, the Romans could produce tiles in great quantities, stockpiling them and letting them dry for as long as a year or even two.

'Right,' says Yalçinkaya. 'And we can't do that, we have a budget and a schedule to meet.'

So in the end, the solution is to have a frame made of steel. To prevent the floor from collapsing, the cracked tiles will be set in the steel frame and the frame will be placed on top of the *pilae*.

Scott is disappointed. 'It's somewhat ironic that my original suggestion to use concrete pavings was dismissed as being inauthentic, and now we've now ended up using these funny things. We've now gone truly inauthentic.'

Max Fordham crawls through the spaces between the pilae *while his assistant, Tristan Couch, looks on.*

'We're learning a lot here, you know,' Rook reminds him.

'We learned something else too,' Yalçinkaya points out. The Romans, he says, were able to obtain much higher quality clay than the NOVA team. In winter, when it rained, the slurry came down to the valley and then the next year, in the springtime, the Romans would take the best part of the slurry and make their clays out of that – the best quality clay to make tiles. As Yalçinkaya says, 'We don't have that chance to do it in time for this project. So this is the result.'

Standing in what will become the *caldarium*, Rook, Fordham and Yegül examine a grid of small brick tiles laid out on the foundation to show where the *pilae* will be placed. Because of the change in the size of the *bipedalis*, the spacing is tight – the pillars will be laid out in rows about 30 cm apart. Still concerned that the close spacing will impede the circulation of the gases, Fordham suggests a change.

'Do you think we can open up a pair so that we get a kind of channel?' he asks. Widening the gap between the two rows of *pilae* leading from the hypocaust to the back of the *caldarium* might have a slight beneficial effect on the flow of heat from the furnace, he says. Moreover, the Romans would have placed the *pilae* far enough apart to allow a slave (probably a child) to crawl through for cleaning purposes. Rook agrees, and demonstrates how the *bipedalis* could be overlapped to allow the two rows of *pilae* to be placed farther apart. Yegül and Yalçinkaya are not convinced that this will affect the heating system, but reluctantly agree to make the change.

But before the workers start to build the *pilae*, Fordham wants to test the newly built furnace and flues to see if they are drawing properly. He uses an

Tristan Couch and Max Fordham on the roof testing the efficiency of the ventilation system.

appropriately low-tech method, holding a sheaf of burning paper to the bottom opening of one of the flues in the *caldarium*. The flame is drawn upward just as it should be, and smoke rises gracefully through the flues to the sky. Then Fordham moves to the inside of the furnace. It, too, seems to operate perfectly, as smoke and flame billow back into the *caldarium*, where the heat from the furnace should be drawn. So the system seems to work – but Fordham reminds the others that it may function very differently once the *pilae* are built and the floor is in place.

With everything set for completion, all the team members except Yalçinkaya take a break from the project and go home to pick up the threads of their daily

lives. They will return in ten days for the final act of the drama: firing the furnace and enjoying their authentic Roman baths.

With the rest of the team gone, Yalçinkaya faces a dilemma. Due partly to the onset of wet weather, the building is not drying as fast as the team planned. There are tons of water in this small building. The bricks of the walls, roofs and hypocaust system are embedded in layer upon layer of mortar. Four inches of wet concrete covers the floors. Wet plaster lines the ceilings and most of the walls; in the baths, a thick layer of wet mortar binds marble panels to the walls and floors.

The building must dry slowly, or else it could shrink and crack. But if the furnace is fired up before the building is dry enough, the heat may cause it to expand and perhaps pull apart. Unlike the Romans, who could let a building dry for weeks or even months, Yalçinkaya has only ten days.

After two days of rain, he makes the risky decision to light the furnace. A small, slow fire, he hopes, might help dry the building without cracking it. Tony Rook's special area of interest is firing the hypocaust – he has even written a paper about it – but he is back in England. In the absence of scholarly expertise, Yalçinkaya turns to an unlikely expert: Ismail Mamak, the village baker, who fires his oven every day.

Marble panelling lines the cold pool in the frigidarium. The thick layers of mortar and concrete used in the NOVA bath took many days to dry.

After surveying the building, the baker agrees to help light the furnace. Yalçinkaya knows the rest of the team will be disappointed – they all wanted to be there for this momentous occasion. On the other hand, if he doesn't get it going, the team will be more disappointed not to have their baths! As Mamak lights the fire, a hundred questions hang silently in the air: will the furnace draw properly? Will the flues vent? Will the walls heat evenly? Will the building crack?

At first, smoke billows out of the furnace. Little of the heat seems to be drawn inside. Yalçinkaya is surprised and a little worried. To help it burn better, Mamak moves the fire deep under the *caldarium*. Soon smoke is pouring from the flues, the walls are warming, and Yalçinkaya breathes a sigh of relief. It will be all right.

When the NOVA team reassembles a few days later, they congratulate Yalçinkaya on his success. The venting system is working, the building is heating, and everything is set for completion. Only the installation of the water boiler remains. And then one final problem surfaces.

The boiler for the NOVA team's bath is modelled after one found in a bath in North Africa, but to the modern eye it looks surprisingly familiar in shape and size, with one pipe connection at the top and two at the sides. As Rook, Scott and Fordham examine it, they become convinced that the system will work more efficiently if the hot water is drawn out from the top of the boiler, rather than from the opening at the side. Otherwise, the hot water above the side opening – about 90 litres – will not be drawn out and refilled. In effect, it will be wasted.

Yalçinkaya is unconcerned. The amount of water below the hole, he says, 'will be sufficient for our purpose'.

Rook interrupts: 'We don't think it will…'

'…because we've calculated the volume of this tank is about 440 litres,' Scott finishes. 'The volume of the bath is about 1800 litres, so this represents something less than a quarter of the volume of the bath. So if you put this amount of hot water, even at 100 degrees Centigrade, into the cold bath, our calculations are that you get a temperature of somewhere in the order of 24 degrees, which isn't sufficient.' The less hot water is drawn from the tank, he explains, the harder it will be to get the baths hot enough.

Yalçinkaya is reluctant to risk rearranging the pipes. 'We're not losing anything,' Rook insists. 'If we're right, then it will work.' When Yegül suggests it may work anyway, he responds: 'I don't think it will.' The debate ignites some long-simmering tensions.

'How can you be so sure?' Yegül asks. 'You know, you had the same reservations and the dire predictions about the whole heating system, you said it wouldn't work, and it's working like a charm.'

'It isn't working yet, because we haven't yet got it working,' Rook insists. 'We haven't put the boiler on yet.'

This is too much for Yegül. 'What do you mean, it isn't working?' he cries.

'We haven't got the building to 50 centigrade yet,' Fordham reminds him gently.

'Who says we have to get to 50 centigrade?' Yegül wheels around. 'Do you know that Roman baths were heated to 50 centigrade? Where do you take that number, out of your hat?'

Fordham keeps his cool. 'No,' he says. 'I take that number out of the American Society of Heating and Refrigeration and Air Conditioning Engineers. It is quite well researched.'

Yegül: 'Turkish baths, which are the closest to Roman baths, never get heated to 50 degrees, never. Forty, I'm with you, but not 50.'

It's a clash of professional perspectives. Yegül, the historian, wants to heat the baths only to the level he considers authentic. Fordham, the engineer, wants to test the heating system to establish the limits of its tolerance. In the end, they reach a compromise: they agree to change the boiler connections, but not to push the building temperature much past 40 degrees.

It takes only a few minutes for the construction crew to put the boiler over an opening in the furnace and connect the pipes. Now it's time for Rook and Scott to move the fire from the middle of the *caldarium* to the front of the furnace, directly under the boiler. The fire will heat the water inside the boiler. But will moving the fire cool down the building? Fordham monitors the temperatures: all seems to be working well.

It takes a whole day for the water to heat up and the baths to fill. The team spends the last night in Turkey having a traditional meal of lamb kebabs, köfte, yogurt and other delicacies. The next day, they'll have the experience they've waited seven weeks and a lifetime to have – a real Roman bath.

But in the morning they discover that while they were sleeping, water was ebbing from the pools in the *caldarium* and *frigidarium*. The mortar at the joints of the marble panelling has cracked – perhaps because the building was heated before the mortar had time to set. There is a solution, but it isn't a Roman one: silicon sealant. The remedy is applied, the tubs are refilled, and finally the baths are ready.

Tony Rook inspects the boiler, used to heat the water for the caldarium *pool.*

One by one the contributors file into the *caldarium.* Immediately they're enveloped in heat – the temperature in the room is about 120 degrees Fahrenheit. In a room that hot, the water of the *caldarium* pool – a mere 100 degrees Fahrenheit – is surprisingly refreshing.

'Ahhhhh, this is a good Roman experience,' says Fagan.

'Push him under and keep him there!' Fordham teases. And Scott replies by dunking Fagan in the pool.

'I'll get you for that!' laughs Fagan.

Like the Romans, they linger in the hot bath until they're completely enervated by the heat. Then it's into the *frigidarium* for a cool dip, some food, drink and a lot of laughter.

In the end, the experience of bathing relaxes any lingering tensions. 'It was wonderful, warm, and pleasant,' Yegül muses afterward. 'There was a wonderful sense of being together in the same small space, all six of us. That's something we don't do in our normal lives – that kind of social togetherness of a Roman bath. We have had different opinions on this and that, about the details of the bath and the technology, but in there, we were all having fun, and that's what a Roman bath is supposed to be.'

Perhaps that's the ultimate secret of the baths – and one reason the Roman civilization lasted for nearly a thousand years.

Below Enjoying a real Roman bath: (left to right) Tony Rook, Garrett Fagan, Fikret Yegül, Bryan Scott, Max Fordham, and Tristan Couch.

Left The caldarium *of the completed NOVA bath boasts a mosaic and cold basin.*

Far left The round pool in the frigidarium *completed and lined with marble.*

Left The fresco adorning the NOVA bath is copied from a late Roman house in Ephesus, Turkey.

5

CHINA
BRIDGE

Just west of Shanghai, 50 miles north of the twelfth-century Song Dynasty capital of Hangzhou, lies the centuries-old town of Jinze. Like many towns in the Yangtze River basin, it is built along a winding canal leading to the river. The heart of the town, with its whitewashed stone and brick houses, tiny kiosks selling everything from vinegar to firecrackers, and vendors on three-wheel bicycle carts, is dominated by this crowded waterway. Pilots use long bamboo poles to guide barges loaded with 100-pound bags of rice or mountains of automobile parts. A woman washes soybeans and water chestnuts in the muddy, greenish water; another rinses her laundry nearby. A young man in a suit walks by them, chatting on his cellphone.

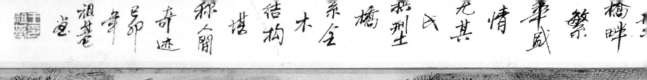

ot far away, at a spot where the canal is about 40 feet wide, a group of workers is pounding 10-foot-long wooden stakes into the bank, using a granite block strapped to four wooden poles as a hammer. They are part of a NOVA expedition that is attempting to construct a rainbow bridge, the most mysterious and perhaps the most beautiful manifestation of medieval China's mastery in bridge building.

During the Song Dynasty (AD 960–1279), as Europe emerged from the Dark Ages, China experienced an efflorescence of science and art. None of this dynasty's engineering achievements surpassed the elegance of its bridges. Described by poets as 'rainbows lying on the waves' or 'turtles' backs reaching the clouds',

medieval Chinese bridges displayed, in the words of historian Joseph Needham, 'a subtle combination of the rational with the romantic'.

The bridges served practical functions as well. In the mountainous southwest, narrow bridges suspended from woven bamboo cables spanned the deep gorges that isolated one hillside village from another. In the coastal southeast, massive granite beams were used to bridge dozens of tidal estuaries. And in the plains of the northeast, crisscrossed by canals and waterways, arched stone and wood bridges – far lighter and more flexible than the arches built in the Roman Empire – allowed people and goods to travel the region on foot or by oxcart. The bridges of the Song Dynasty enhanced a bustling commercial life in towns across the land, part of a complex infrastructure that promoted unprecedented prosperity and technological advancement.

The rainbow bridge is the most innovative of these lightweight arched bridges. Unlike any kind of bridge known in the West, it uses short pieces of timber that are actually woven over and under a series of cross-beams and lashed together with bamboo straps. Topped with a railing that has a graceful 'reverse curve' (the railing curves over the top of the bridge with a little dip on either side), the bridge soars across the water unsupported by piers.

This unique and mysterious bridge is known to history only through a single image: it catches the eye as a tiny detail on a famous scroll painting called 'Going Up the River During the Qingming Festival' by the twelfth-century court painter Zhang Zeduan. No pure rainbow bridges survive today; no one knows how they were built or even what engineering principles underlay their design.

The NOVA team brings together an international assortment of engineers, architects, historians and carpenters with the quixotic mission to recreate this long-vanished work of art and science. All they have to guide them are the thousand-year-old scroll painting; a man who has devoted his life to the study of ancient bridges, in particular the one in that painting; and their own wits.

Legend has it that the Sage Emperor Yu created the first bridge in China around the beginning of the third millennium BC, when he ordered giant turtles to align themselves in a river in such a way that he might cross it. The earliest Chinese bridges either inspired or drew inspiration from this tale: even today one can find many shallow streams with stones positioned in them as natural walkways, still called 'turtle bridges'.

Some time after Yu's era, simple wooden beam bridges – logs or sets of logs laid across streams – appeared. Around 1000 BC King Wen, who founded the Zhou dynasty, ordered workers to build a pontoon bridge across the Wei River in northwest China. It was made of a series of boats anchored side by side with planks laid over them. Later, beam bridges were built from massive granite slabs. In the third century BC the first suspension bridges appeared in southwest China. At first suspended from cables made of plaited bamboo, these bridges were later supported by iron chains – a thousand years before the same technology appeared in Europe. The first arched bridges appeared in China in the third century BC as well, around the same time as they made their appearance in the Roman Empire, but using a uniquely Chinese approach. In 221 BC, Emperor Qin Shi Huangdi ordered the construction of a stone arch bridge 54 feet wide and more than 14,000 feet long, involving 68 arches, 750 piers and 220 beams.

Finally, in the fourth century AD, Chinese engineers devised the cantilever bridge. In this type, an arm extends from each bank, supported by an abutment of piled stone or masonry. These arms could be joined by a simple beam, or else another type of bridge could be built between them. Over the next fifteen centuries, the Chinese continued to lead the world in developing their bridge-making techniques.

The leader of the NOVA team, Tang Huan Cheng, has been building bridges since he graduated from Shanghai National University in 1948 and joined the new China Bridge Company, which was formed to repair and replace bridges destroyed in the war with Japan. A few years later, he won first prize in a national design competition for a new bridge to be built over the Yangtze River at Nanjing. Around the same time, the new communist government nationalized his company, and Tang found himself an engineer of the Ministry of Railways.

In the 1950s Tang began researching ancient bridges as a way of trying to define a Chinese 'national style', which the communist regime had mandated for all new bridges. Tang took to the new task, and ancient bridges became a career interest. Over the decades, he has crisscrossed his vast country, examining extant bridges, remains of ruined ones and the geology of their sites to determine how and why certain types of bridges were built in certain places. His seminal book, *China's Ancient Bridges*, originally published in 1958, will be reissued this year in a 660,000-word third edition boasting more than 900 photographs.

One of the greatest examples of Chinese engineering prowess is the Anlan suspension bridge, first built in the third century BC in Sichuan province. Because of the thousand-foot width of the Min River at that spot, the bridge consists of eight spans separated by supporting piers. Originally built with bamboo ropes and wooden supports, the Anlan bridge has been rebuilt several times over the centuries and is still in use today, with steel cables and concrete trestles. (It is near one of China's most famous engineering projects, the Duiang Yan, where in the third century BC the Qin governor Li Bing had workers cut through a mountain to control the flooding of the Min River and irrigate the central Sichuan plain. This waterway is still in use today and has permitted the population of Sichuan to grow to 100 million.)

The Anlan suspension bridge, first built in the third century B.C., has been rebuilt numerous times over the centuries. Its bamboo ropes and wooden supports have been replaced with steel cables and concrete trestles; the bridge is still well used today.

To introduce the NOVA team to the challenges involved in building a suspension bridge, Tang leads them on a side trip to Yixian, in the south-central province of Anhui, where they will try to build their own suspension bridge using traditional bamboo cables. It's October, rice-harvesting season in Anhui province, and the fields are covered with conical piles of rice stalks. The villagers are consumed with the task of winnowing and drying the rice on bamboo mats.

The NOVA team threads its way through the narrow streets that vein the ancient towns of this region and drive up to the narrow gorge that will be its building site. Imposing limestone walls frame a clear green stream that irrigates the rice fields above and below it. Just before they reach the site, the team passes a chain-link suspension bridge. A small elderly man sits inside a small shack next to it. Zhan Peijun was once the town lawyer, but now he devotes himself to this spot above the river. His bridge is a small-time tourist attraction; for a few pennies, he allows customers to make their rickety way 60 feet above the river. His latest project

Zhan Peijun operates this chain-link suspension bridge in Yixian as a tourist attraction.

Altabba looks on glumly as workers try to disentangle the rolled-up rope bridge.

is just down the road, where he has strung three steel cables across the gorge and attached a small metal cage cloaked in red velvet. Zhan intends his spot to be a sort of Niagara Falls of Yixian; here newlyweds can pull themselves across the gorge using a simple pulley system to enjoy the honeymoon suite he has built in a grotto in the cliffs on the far side. But he is still waiting for his first newlywed customers.

The NOVA team continues on to the site. Marcus Brandt, a stonemason and timber framer from Pennsylvania, has already been there for two days, overseeing the installation of the anchoring system. Brandt has extensive experience working with historical construction techniques and brings a repertoire of practical solutions to the project. On the far side, two stakes are already in place, buried two feet deep in solid rock. The ropes from which one end of the bridge will hang will be tied to these. On the near side, workers begin to pound a timber into a crevice between the rocks under the direction of Brandt, Tang, and Bashar Altabba, a structural engineer from MIT who brings a more theoretical orientation to the project. The timber protrudes almost horizontally from the crevice.

Altabba doesn't think the foundation is secure. At Brandt's suggestion, seven workers lever a heavy rock on to the timber to ensure its stability. This will serve as the anchor for the other end of the bridge. 'You could hang the world on that,' Brandt says cheerfully.

With the anchors firmly in place, the NOVA team rides out to another small village, really just a narrow stone alley lined with a few ancient homes. Here lives a man who makes bamboo rope. For the benefit of his visitors, he demonstrates how to weave the long thin strips together into a 2-inch-thick rope. Tang has already tested this type of rope back in Shanghai. It took a stress of 9530 pounds per square inch to break it, which compares quite favourably with the 8000-psi limit for 2-inch hemp rope. And for this bridge, three ropes have been braided together to give the cable extra strength.

The bamboo cables are stored underwater to keep them supple. The next day, local workers lay out the two longest cables side by side. Shorter cross-ropes, which will support the decking, are knotted to them at either end, spaced about a yard apart like rungs on a ladder. The plan is to roll up the completed bridge, tie one end to one of the anchors, and simply unroll it across the gorge. This is Altabba's idea, as a way to avoid having to attach the cross-ropes while hanging above the surface of the fast-moving river.

Unfortunately, when they start to unfurl the rolled-up bridge, the cables become hopelessly tangled, like a necklace knotted up at the bottom of a jewellery box. Altabba paces back and forth, watching helplessly as the workers try to straighten out the strands. 'It was going so well,' he moans. 'When I see how this thing is unravelling, I just want to cry.'

Finally, the crew gets the bridge untangled, and a shout of joy erupts. The workers anchor the two long cables at one end to the two stakes on one bank. They tie a rope to the cables at the other end and haul the rope bridge across the gorge by boat. There the far ends of the two long cables are pulled over the top of a wooden M-shaped frame and anchored to the timber wedged into the rock behind it. At Brandt's suggestion, the crew uses a device called a Spanish windlass to tighten the cables, winding them around a capstan to hoist the bridge above the water. Finally the bridge, minus planking, is up.

When the NOVA team comes back in the early morning, the middle of the bridge has vanished behind a thick fog that has slipped in from the mountain range. Down in the gorge, ghostly figures wander around on the banks. Altabba insists that it is too dangerous to lay the planking until the fog lifts. Within a few hours, the view is clear. Workers balance above the water on the suspended cables, laying the planking in place and lashing the segments together with bamboo rope. Now the bridge is complete. But is it strong enough?

The NOVA team has calculated that the bridge should be able to bear twelve people. Before testing the bridge, some of the local workers set off long strings of firecrackers on a flat rock near the bridge to ward off bad spirits. Explosions echo off the walls of the gorge, and red paper and smoke fill the air. Brandt and Xu Cheng Song, the foreman, step on to the bridge from opposite sides and gingerly make their way towards the centre. The bridge sways perilously, but holds. When they meet in the middle, the two men shake hands and let out a shout. The rest of the chosen dozen file on to the bridge, entering two by two from opposite sides.

The NOVA team places the braided bamboo cables that will support the suspension bridge over the M-shaped wooden frame on one side of the gorge.

As the last two people step on to the deck, there is a loud pop. Everyone freezes. The M-shaped frame is listing towards the water. Hurriedly, the group files back off the bridge. Once everyone is safely ashore, Tang explains calmly, 'The cable is OK, the deck is OK, but maybe the portal [M-shaped frame] is sloped too much toward the river.' He suggests that the frame be tilted back to better support the bridge.

Though the humble new bridge in Yixian may not inspire soaring poetry, it is enough to suggest the beauty and grace of the ancient suspension bridges. Grateful to be back on solid ground, the NOVA team develops a new respect for the ingenuity of the bridgemakers over 2000 years ago who first made it possible to walk through the air on hanging ropes of bamboo.

The ingenuity of Chinese bridge builders found perhaps its greatest expression in their use of the arch. Leonardo da Vinci described an arch as two weaknesses which, leaning on each other, become a strength. In an arch, the weight of the load – say, a cart travelling over it – is converted from a weight pointing straight downward into forces that travel outward along the curve of the arch. This force, known as axial compression, is carried into the ground at either end.

The Romans built enormous, semicircular arches of solid stone, supported by equally massive stone piers on either side. But the Chinese, who developed the arch independently in the third century BC, had to find a different solution. The banks of their rivers were soft and giving, so they couldn't build foundations as heavy as the Romans'. Instead, Chinese engineers built small piers and constructed their arches out of thin, hollow shells filled with loose rubble. These lightweight arches were wonderfully flexible and could span as much as 65 feet each. Arranged in multiple-arch bridges, they could cover great distances.

The most revolutionary of China's stone arch bridges is the Zhaozhou (or Anji 'Safe Crossing') Bridge, built in the northeastern province of Hebei at the beginning of the seventh century AD. One of the world's engineering landmarks, it was the first segmental-arch bridge ever built, appearing 740 years before the first western segmental arch (the Ponte Vecchio in Florence, built in 1345). Li Chun, the architect believed to have designed the bridge, was apparently the first to realize that a full semicircle was not needed to withstand the vertical force of the

Twelve people file onto the NOVA suspension bridge to test its load-bearing capacity.

load. The great Zhaozhou Bridge, then, describes a shallower curve, a single 118-foot span that allows for a gradual approach while offering ample room beneath for maritime traffic.

Li Chun introduced another important advance in the design of the bridge's spandrels – the area between the arch and the upper roadway at either end. By opening up each spandrel with a pair of small arches, he made the entire bridge lighter and more flexible, and he provided a vent for flood waters to pass through, making the bridge more stable in storms. Open spandrels like this were not seen in the West until the nineteenth century.

The Zhaozhou Bridge remained the longest single-arch bridge in China until the mid-twentieth century. To this day it is regarded as one of China's principal contributions to world architecture. As Bashar Altabba points out, the construction of the Zhaozhou Bridge 'was the first time in history where there was a clear engineering consciousness of the concept of forces'. The bridge builders, he says, 'were not saying that from experience, we know if we pile a bunch of stones they will all stand up. Somebody was actually sitting and thinking about which part of the stone is doing the work and which is not. And from there comes the idea of the open spandrel.

'It's so elegant. It's so beautiful. It could be called structural art. It's not just about building a bridge – it's about building an elegant, economic, and efficient structure.'

The Zhaozhou was completed in AD 605, near the end of the short-lived Sui Dynasty (581–618) and just before the ascension of the Tang (618–906). The great innovations in bridge engineering during the Sui and Tang dynasties were only one facet of a period of burgeoning creativity and change that would reach its apotheosis during the Song Dynasty.

One of the great contributions of the Sui and Tang was the use of free examinations to choose officials for the civil service. Government officials were

The Zhaozhou (or Anji 'Safe Crossing') Bridge was the first segmented-arch bridge ever built. Note the open spandrels – the small arches set into the area between the arch and the upper roadway.

hired on the basis of their scores to administer the empire that was then the largest in the world. Previously, one could enter the imperial service only through birthright or high connections. The use of examinations transformed the aristocracy into a bureaucratic meritocracy. The Tang also introduced a more efficient system of revenue collection and conducted accurate censuses (the count for AD 745: 52,880,488).

'Examination of the Letters by Jint Song.' This eighteenth-century watercolour depicts the Song emperor reviewing civil service examination papers. Song government officials were chosen on the basis of examination results, rather than hereditary privilege or political connections.

The Tang was a highly cosmopolitan society. Members of the scholar-elite patronized the Buddhist and Daoist churches, and Islam and variant forms of Christianity were introduced from the West through the Silk Road. The scholars' dedication to learning and literature, especially poetry, paved the way for the intellectual achievements of the Song.

During its last half-century, though, the Tang Dynasty fell into a state of chaos. From 906 on, China was split into various states, each ruled by its own self-declared 'emperor'. One night in 960, the commander of the palace guard under a child emperor was roused by his officers and coerced into becoming emperor. Zhao Kuangyin accepted the Mandate of Heaven and thus became the founder of the Song Dynasty. He and his able successors restored the cultural glory of the Chinese empire but were never able to recover all the territory ruled by the Tang.

Once again the civil service ruled supreme, as the finest minds in the land presided over a medieval economic revolution. Urban life thrived as the capital, Kaifeng, swelled to three times the size of ancient Rome, with a population of over a million. Vast deposits of coal were used in coke-burning blast furnaces to produce cast iron, which Song ironworkers turned into steel using their new carbonization methods. This in turn sparked military innovations, such as coats of chain mail and steel swords. The Song also pioneered the use of gunpowder in cannon, mines, grenades, bombs and fire-lances.

Their innovations had peaceable uses as well. The Song modernized silkmaking by improving silk-reeling methods and developing complex looms, such as the jacquard loom used to weave silk brocade. Some of these looms required as many as 1800 different parts.

Robin Yates, a professor of Chinese history at McGill University, who is on hand to advise the NOVA team, calls the Song Dynasty 'the first information age'. Long before Gutenberg's invention of movable type in the fifteenth century, the Song's woodblock printing techniques – well suited to Chinese ideogrammatic characters – fomented the first widespread use of books. Government policies supported the popularization of printing and a private publishing industry began to flourish.

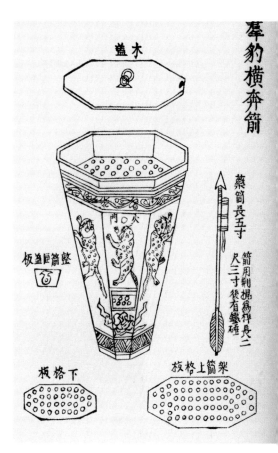

'The invention of printing revolutionized education in society,' Yates explains. 'The government printed medical texts and agricultural manuals and distributed them among the people. For the scholars, they printed Confucian texts, and they also printed technical manuals and encyclopedias, such as the one that contains the formula for gunpowder.'

Another important text was the Song Dynasty building manual, the *Ying Tsao Fa Shih (Construction Principles)*. Printed by the central government's Board of Works in 1103, it consolidated a set of building standards that would be maintained into the twentieth century. A Song-era client could order a park pavilion, a warehouse or a palace hall in any size, and the carpenters would have a blueprint to ensure quality control. Aside from practical matters, the manual also dictated which symbolic decorations should be included, such as the standard lion-

This gunpowder rocket launcher was one of many military technologies introduced in the Song dynasty.

seated-on-lotus-pedestal motif and the dragon, the symbol of natural forces. The designs in the *Ying Tsao Fa Shih* were not necessarily invented during the Song Dynasty, but it was then that they were preserved for centuries to come.

There were fewer revolts during the Song than in any other dynasty. The Song's problem was fighting off foreign invaders, which may seem surprising considering their impressive new military technologies. The problem was that the Song had to rely on their enemies – nomads to the north and northwest – for their supply of cavalry horses. Because China was ecologically unsuited to raising these animals, Song armies were always less mobile than those of their adversaries. Moreover, the empire's scholar—statesmen did not always agree on what policy to adopt to keep these enemies at bay.

Virtually all followed the ideals of Confucius, whose philosophy underwent a strong revival during the Song era. Neo-Confucianism, a hybrid of Confucianism and Buddhist transcendentalism, became the guiding philosophy of the Chinese elite well into the twentieth century. The neo-Confucian scholar–statesmen considered it their responsibility to take care of the country, morally and economically. As the philosopher Fan Zhongyan put it, 'Before the rest of the world starts worrying, the scholar worries; after the rest of the world rejoices, he rejoices.'

But neo-Confucianism regarded the military with a near disdain, considering it nothing more than a necessary evil. Unfortunately, it was a very necessary evil. The Chinese emperors, for whom the neo-Confucian bureaucrats worked, needed a powerful army to preserve the empire. Nomadic tribesmen who roamed Inner Asia were constantly threatening China's borders, and in the end their ruthless militarism would take advantage of the Song's enlightened pacifism.

The Song Dynasty presents an unusual instance of a civilization thriving economically, intellectually, and in the popularity of its monarch, while at the same time facing gradual invasion by foreign forces. Not often is a country conquered during its finest hour.

It happened in two stages. In 1125 Ruzhen (also called Jurchen) nomads from northern Manchuria seized the state of Liao, which lay directly north of the

This detail of a scroll painting by the Song emperor Hui Tsung, copied from an earlier work, shows court ladies preparing newly woven silk. In 1126, Hui lost the northern Song empire to Jurchen nomads from the north.

Song and included Beijing and part of the Great Wall. The Song were immobilized by divisive debate: should they appease the Ruzhen, ceding them land in exchange for peace, or fight them to the death? Surely with their innovative new weapons of steel and gunpowder they could resist savages on horseback. Unfortunately, though, Chinese scientific advances had already reached Manchuria, and the barbarians at the gate had gunpowder and bombs of their own. And the Song emperor, Hui Tsung, an artist of great renown, was not much interested in matters political or military.

While the scholar–statesmen debated and the emperor painted, Chinese forces suffered defeat after defeat. In 1126 the invaders seized the capital of Kaifeng as well as the emperor Hui and his son, the heir apparent, and what remained of the Song court fled south. They established a new capital at Hangzhou, which eventually grew to a city every bit as impressive as Kaifeng. In 1142, the new Southern Song government officially ceded North China to the Ruzhen by treaty, agreeing to be vassal of and pay annual tribute to the Jin ('Golden') Dynasty (the Ruzhen's new name). For the first time ever, a considerable portion of the Chinese people was now ruled by foreigners.

The Northern Song Dynasty, 960—1126, was over. But the Southern Song would sneer at military defeat and flourish for another 150 years. Hangzhou would grow into the world's largest city, its twenty miles along the Qiantang River home to over a million people.

The Song economy exploded in the south, largely because of advances in agriculture. By the thirteenth century, China had the most sophisticated agricultural system in the world, highlighted by their mastery of wet-field rice cultivation. Farmers learned to plant seedlings in seedbeds before setting them out in the paddies and to prepare their soil much more effectively. The manure business boomed. Mud was also a valuable fertilizer, as the poet Mao Hsu reflected:

The scoopnets with their bamboo arms
Lift mud from the river.
The richest mud
Comes from the creeks around the city.
Fully laden, the boats return
To where the sowing's done,
Like traders back
From commerce in the south.

Into their newly enriched soil the Song farmers sowed a variety of new improved strains of seed. The new rices were drought-resistant and were low in gluten, ripened faster, and grew in poorer soils. Cultivation was now a yearlong process, eliminating seasonal unemployment and creating a surplus that bolstered economic growth. In addition, farmers mastered new methods of double cropping: farming different types of crops side by side. To invigorate their all-season farms, the Chinese developed new hydraulic techniques, building new dams, polders (circular dykes as large as 28 miles in circumference), and reservoirs, and dredging and even rerouting rivers.

The Southern Song made it an official policy to encourage small farmers to embrace the new progressive techniques. The advent of printed books made it easier for the government to disseminate this knowledge. And as commerce expanded, highlighted by the introduction of paper currency, subsistence-based farming gave way to a complex agricultural economy based on crop specialization. Rather than simply growing food for their own use, farmers produced whatever crop was best

suited to their particular soil or would fetch the best price in the market. Village markets were linked into local and regional trade networks and farmers were even able to sell their produce for international export.

This expansion of trade was made possible by advances in transportation as impressive as those in agriculture. The state maintained old roads and built great highways paved in stone or brick. Officials even planted trees along roadsides to provide travellers with shady resting spots.

The great highways of commerce, however, were the inland rivers and canals. The Grand Canal, built in the seventh century, provided a north—south link between the Yangtze and Yellow River basins, allowing local economies to expand into national ones. By the time of the Song, southern and central China were veined with a complex web of waterways. The invention of the double lock in the eleventh century eased passage past difficult points and also enabled ships five times as large to pass. The poet Yuan Chüeh wrote:

> *The boats of the Yellow River are like slices of cut melon*
> *Covered with iron nails for scraping the sandy shallows…*
> *With the wind set fair, a thousand sails*
> *Will move at different speeds…*

Marco Polo, a native of Venice, the greatest seaport in Europe, wrote home from the city of I-ching:

> *I assure you that this river runs for such a distance and through so many regions and there are so many cities on its banks that truth to tell, in the amount of shipping it carries and the total volume and value of its traffic, it exceeds all the rivers of the Christians put together and their seas into the bargain. I give you my word that I have seen in this city fully five thousand ships at once, all afloat on this river. Then you may reflect, since this city, which is not very big, has so many ships, how many there must be in the others. For I assure you that the river flows through more than sixteen provinces, and there are on its banks more than two hundred cities, all having more ships than this.*

Bridges formed the joints of this elaborate skeleton of roads and waterways. The Song Dynasty was a period of extraordinary bridge-building. Two stone beam bridges are particularly noteworthy. The An Ping Bridge in Fujien Province, about 18 miles southwest of Quanzhou, is one of the era's most remarkable achievements. Built in 1138, its 331 stone piers support stone beams that span a 6600-foot length of the South China Sea. The longest of the stone beam bridges, it is still in use today.

The Wanan (or Luoyang) Bridge, built in 1053–9 near the important southeastern seaport of Quanzhou, comprised 35-foot-long granite slabs forming forty-seven spans stretching over 3500 feet. It is said that the engineers used the ebb and flow of the tides to help position the slabs. They also apparently used living oysters as a natural mastic to fasten the crevices of a stone foundation that ran from shore to shore. Much of the original foundation remains, underneath a concrete causeway built in the 1930s.

The rainbow bridge is a smaller, more subtle example of the Song engineers' ingenuity. In the interior regions, the heart of river-based commerce, people needed a way to cross the canals of the towns and cities, filled with barges, sailboats and rowboats, without disrupting traffic. Here, bridge builders built only with wood. They needed a lightweight design and a high clearance, like that of an arch, to let boats pass underneath. The rainbow bridge was apparently the perfect solution.

Official historians of the Song Dynasty credited Governor Xiliang Chen with the invention of the rainbow bridge, but the real architect is unknown. In the late eleventh century, a writer from Qingzhou (present-day Yidu in Shandong province) wrote of his town's Yang River:

> *Originally timber bridges spanned the river, but when the waters swelled in June and July the piers were frequently damaged and the town greatly disrupted. In the Mingdao reign [1032–33]... there was a certain retired prison guard who was known for his ingenuity; he piled*

up large stones to secure the abutments, and then by connecting a score of great beams together, he threw across the river a flying bridge that had no central piers. It has stood for fifty years and remained undamaged. In the Qingli reign [1041–8]… the bridges on the Bien Canal were in such a state of disrepair that they often interfered with official transportation and even caused loss of life, so flying bridges like those in Qingzhou were built. Nowadays the bridges between the Fen River and the Bien Canal are all flying bridges, to the great benefit of communication. They are commonly called 'rainbow bridges'.

From the few extant historical writings, we know that the rainbow bridge in the scroll painting was built in AD 1032 in the northern capital of Kaifeng, over the Bien Canal – the grand waterway that brought grain, particularly rice, up from the southeast. 'Seven *li* [624 yards] outside of the east gate stood the Rainbow Bridge,' wrote one Southern Song historian. 'The bridge had no piers, but giant timbers spanned the void, decorated with red paint and curved like a rainbow. Upstream and downstream from it all the local bridges were like this…'

As with the Egyptian obelisks (see Chapter 2), no technical information is included in the historical texts that mention rainbow bridges. 'The histories of the region were written by scholars, not specialists in technology,' notes Yates. 'They had little interest in how exactly bridges were built. And the rainbow bridge in the painting is the only surviving picture.' Realistic pictures from that era are very rare, he adds, so the scroll painting is especially useful.

To complicate matters, some versions of the scroll painting do not show the rainbow bridge at all. One, dating from the Ming Dynasty, shows a stone arch bridge instead. But it also features horses, indicating that it is a later version. Tang Huan Cheng points out, however, that Zhang Zeduan, the painter of the original scroll, was a member of the court of the emperor Hui Zheng. And Hui Zheng was very strict about having things represented accurately.

'He himself was a painter of birds and flowers, and he painted them exquisitely, with exquisite detail,' Tang notes. 'The painting itself is in exquisite detail, with more than a thousand figures. If a painter represented a bird lifting his left foot, and Hui Zheng said no, it was his right foot, he would have to go and paint it again.' Using the scroll painting and his slide rule, Tang tried to determine the bridge's technical specifications.

'I studied the size of the bridge by looking at the people on the bridge railing,' he recalls. 'Judging by the size of the human beings, there were 0.8 metres between the railing panels, and within the span of the bridge, there were 24 panels, so that means the bridge span was about 19.2 metres. Then I found out that the Bien River was a bit more than 15 metres. So the bridge spans 19 metres and the river width is 15 metres – that's a very reasonable estimation.' Using similar estimates based on the weight of 'peace cars' shown in the painting – carts pulled by oxen and braked by donkeys in the rear – he figured that the bridge had about a 3-ton capacity.

But how exactly were these bridges constructed? And, more mysterious, how did the builders manage to put them in place over the river without stifling river traffic for weeks or months? There were no bridge engineers at that time, with a scientific method to solve the problem. Instead, there were skilful and sometimes ingenious carpenters, or craftsmen, who would design a new bridge through experience and intuition.

'The way we're attacking this problem here is the way it must've been attacked during the Song period,' says Tom Peters, head of the architecture department of the Chinese University of Hong Kong, a specialist in historical construction techniques and an adviser to the NOVA team. 'When this bridge was first conceived, it had never been done before. That's how it is now. So we're attacking the problem intellectually, exactly the same way the builders attacked it in the Song. And that's the exciting thing. We're learning how these people thought.'

They do, however, have a few real bridges to study – not true rainbow bridges, but later structures that evolved from them. For this the team can thank Tang Huan Cheng. In 1981, while working in the back country of Zhejiang province, he came across the Mei Chong Bridge, which had long been classified as a beam bridge. Upon inspecting it closely, he was amazed to find its internal structure to be closely related to the rainbow bridge.

Eighteen years later, Tang leads the NOVA team on a trek into the interior to examine the Xi Dong Bridge, another bridge closely related to the rainbow bridge that he discovered in 1992, which he considers the most beautiful of its kind. From the port town of Wenzhou, they wind and bump for more than six hours along mountainous dirt roads. They pass terraced rice fields, tea bushes, bamboo thickets, and village after village, most of them no more than a few mud-and-brick huts. Finally they arrive in the town of Sixi, a larger development with many new buildings, although most of them remain unfinished, lacking windows and doors. Behind the main road, between the schoolhouse and the mountains, lies the Xi Dong Bridge.

At first glance it looks nothing like the original rainbow bridge: the dominant feature is an elaborate tiled roof with dragons dancing along the top. Red planking along the sides blocks the view of the deck. The walkway appears flat: no swooping curve.

But Tang leads the group under the bridge, and there the underlying structure is revealed – the intricate weave of wooden beams into a graceful arch that is the hallmark of the rainbow bridge. Closer inspection, however, illuminates several key differences. For one thing, this bridge uses mortise-and-tenon joints instead of bamboo rope to hold the beams together which are supported at the lower end by short stone posts.

'You see,' explains Tang, 'the original style is from northern carpenters, but improvements were made by southern carpenters after the Song moved south. For instance, Southern Song bridges always have these covering structures. So the rainbow-type bridges we now find in the south are combinations.'

Tang found another close cousin of the rainbow bridge at Weiyuan, in southern Gansu province. Built in 1919, the Baling Bridge was patterned after the Wo (Lying) Bridge, which was built in the same town during the Tang Dynasty and finally dismantled a thousand years later, in the 1950s. The Baling Bridge appears to be a hybrid of a cantilever bridge and a rainbow bridge. Eleven sets of beams are cantilevered out from each abutment, and the gap between them is spanned by what looks like a rainbow bridge. In fact, though, even the centre section is not strictly a rainbow bridge, as it is held together by pegs instead of woven short timbers. And in this case the southern-style arcade over the entire structure changes the dynamic of the combined forces, taking some load off of the cantilevered sections.

Tang found many other suspects that proved to be close to Kaifeng's Rainbow Bridge, but apparently the real thing no longer exists. Today, Tang and the other NOVA team members in Jinze are still trying to recreate the object of their search. By compiling all the related information that they can, they hope to fulfil Tang's dream of building an authentic rainbow bridge.

Back in Jinze, local Chinese workers stand knee deep in mud as they continue pounding the wooden spikes into the wet banks on either side of the bridge. Light rain is occasionally interrupted by sunny breaks and warm breezes. The crew of four men and two women are building the abutments, or foundations, for the bridge. Thirty-six of the wooden spikes, called piles, will form the bottom layer of each abutment. The workers bang the piles into a large hole they have dug on each side of the canal. A long, narrow coffer dam two or three feet high is constructed around the hole to keep the water from flowing in. The coffer dam is made of a double wall of bamboo mats set in the canal bottom. As mud is scooped out of the hole, it is dumped between the mats to form a dam. Eventually, the piles will rest below water. Since it is the mixture of moisture and air that rots wood, the piles will be protected under water and can last for centuries.

Once the thirty-six piles are in place, the workers begin the next layer, placing stone blocks on top of the timber. After that, they pile on a layer of rubble fill, followed by another layer of stone, like a great rubble-and-rock lasagne. Workers sling bamboo poles over their shoulders to transport blocks of granite and pails of rubble around the work site, negotiating their way across precarious paths wearing worn-out flimsy tennis shoes, or even flip-flops. As the abutments grow, friends and neighbours gather on the banks to watch, munching on sunflower seeds and dried salty soybeans. Finally, the workers seal each abutment in a huge stone box, made of granite slabs, as tall and wide as three stacked cars.

When Altabba, Yates and Tang arrive on the scene, they are not pleased with what they see. 'This is a serious problem,' says Altabba. 'If we build the bridge on it now, it's going to collapse!' That design, he explains, called for the stones to be interlocked horizontally and vertically, in order to handle both the horizontal and vertical components of the stress. But the Chinese contractor built the abutments before the NOVA team arrived. To make things easier for his crew, he had them lay all the stones flat, with rubble in between, but with no vertical pieces.

'It's a shame we didn't see this earlier,' Altabba continues. 'The only part taking the thrust will be a thin layer of stone on top. And that layer can slide off because it's not connected.'

Tom Peters is also on hand. He emphasizes how important foundations are to a bridge, or any other structure. Usually it's the clients who fail to understand this and are reluctant to pay for the proper construction. In this case, however, the problem is the opposite: it's the contractor who wanted to cut corners. Altabba reminds him that it's also common for the contractor to try to finish the job before the engineer can inspect it.

Protected by a coffer dam, workers drive spikes into the ground to lay the abutments for the NOVA rainbow bridge.

What then, to do? If Altabba is right, and the foundation as it is cannot support the bridge, then it must be fixed somehow. The contractor, meanwhile, insists that the abutments are fine. The irony of the situation is that the foundation is strong enough to support a small high-rise: the layers of flat stone can handle an enormous weight, as long as all the stress is vertical. But they may not be able to support this small wooden bridge because it converts the load into a partly horizontal force.

NOVA team member Andrew Li, a professor of architecture at Hong Kong University and an expert in traditional Song carpentry, is not worried. 'Bashar is talking about a worst-case scenario,' he says. 'So maybe we should just take them at their word and get on with it.'

To placate the westerners, the contractor promises to reinforce the abutments overnight by bracing them with vertical stones. The NOVA experts accept his offer and move forward with the building of the bridge.

The next day, timber framer Marcus Brandt arrives. He has devised his own strategy for building the rainbow bridge and hopes to persuade the NOVA team to use it. On hearing of the problems with the abutments, Brandt is unconcerned. 'This bridge is as much a beam as an arch, according to the models I've built and played with,' he declares. 'Once it locks together the thrust is pretty much straight down and not too much out.'

He is reopening an ongoing argument with Altabba that began back in the States. Altabba has analysed the rainbow bridge by creating a computer model of it and subjecting the model to virtual loads. 'At first the question of what type of bridge it is was very much up for debate,' he says. 'But now I'm convinced that the rainbow bridge acts like a pure arch.'

Before the project, Altabba showed his students at MIT the computer model in action. First he showed them a model of an arch bridge, and then he applied a typical load. The picture of the arch dipped down in the middle and kicked out at the sides. Then he presented the model of the rainbow bridge. When the load was applied, it acted exactly the same as the arch.

'An arch takes its force as pure compression,' he explained. 'That's what you're seeing here. The rainbow bridge does the same thing. Some people called it a beam-arch because it is constructed of straight pieces. That is, it is an arch made out of beams. But as far as how it *acts*, it is an arch.'

The debate over the classification of the rainbow bridge will continue throughout the project. It is more than semantic, for whether or not the compromised abutments will support the bridge depends on how the bridge converts the force of the load. The question, though, will be decided empirically, as the NOVA team has decided simply to put the bridge up and see what happens. For now the only decision to be made is what method of construction they are going to use to put the thing up.

The bridge consists of a four-sided arch woven into a three-sided arch. The first element to be erected is the three-sided arch. Once it is in place, the four-sided arch will be woven into it beam by beam. Finally, the curved planking of the roadway will be laid down.

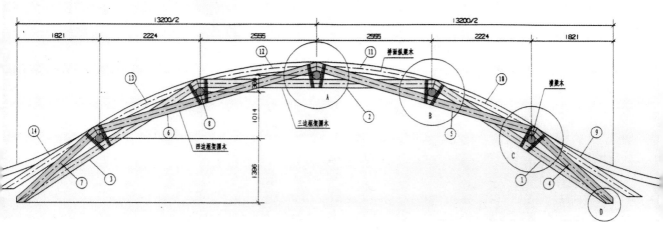

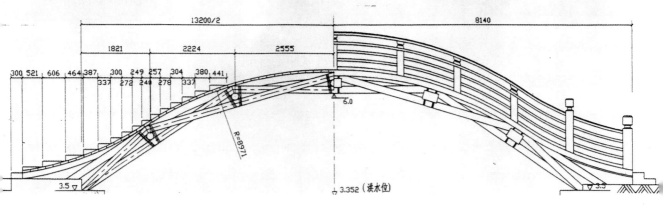

The trickiest part is building the three-sided arch across the river. Three methods have been proposed. Tang, together with his colleague Yang Shijin, a bridge specialist from the Tongji University engineering school, has suggested that the Song builders must have used barges in the water to get construction started. Tang points out that the rainbow bridge in the Zheng painting was built over a slow-flowing river, where barges would be feasible.

Tang and Yang plan to float the timbers for the centre section of the three-sided arch into the middle of the canal on a boat. When assembled, the centre section will look from above like a big H. The two side sections, also resembling large Hs, will be constructed on opposite banks and hoisted out over the river, using a block-and-tackle system. Once the side sections are in place, workers standing in the boat will attach the beams for the centre section to the two sides.

Altabba and Brandt have a problem with the Chinese proposal. They say that there is evidence that some rainbow bridges were built over deep ravines, rapids or

Tang's blueprints for the construction of the NOVA rainbow bridge show the complex interweaving of the three-sided arch (top) and the graceful reverse curve of the railing (bottom).

3-sided arch

4-sided arch

cross beams and lashing

heavily trafficked waterways, where raising the centre section from a boat would not have been feasible. Therefore, there must have been a system for erecting rainbow bridges entirely from the banks. The Mei Chong Bridge, for instance, is high above a river so rough that Tang and Yang's method would have been out of the question.

Both Altabba's and Brandt's proposals involve building the entire bridge on shore and then putting it in place over the river without actually getting into the water. Altabba's plan is to assemble half of the bridge on each bank and then use pulleys to lower each side over the river like a drawbridge, bringing the two halves together. Brandt wants to build the entire bridge on one side, fold it inward accordion-style, and then deploy it across the river in much the same way as one might raise the cloth roof on a convertible car. He later modifies his plan so that only part of the bridge would be deployed this way.

Each candidate builds a small wooden model to demonstrate his plan, and the entire crew gathers to adjudicate.

'I don't know,' says Altabba after Tang's demonstration. 'I think the geometry makes it very difficult.' He notes that the interwoven beams must be joined very precisely in order for the bridge to support itself. 'We tried to build two large-scale models at home, and I was astounded by the difficulty of making the rainbow geometry work. And that was just building a model on dry land.'

Engineer Bashar Altabba (centre) demonstrates his plan for building the rainbow bridge while timber framer Marcus Brandt (right) and professor of architecture Andrew Li (left) look on.

Along with Brandt and Li, Altabba is concerned about the stability of the three-part apparatus called for in Tang and Yang's plan. After all, they wouldn't want to be the ones lashing poles on the half-finished structure 16 feet above the water. Yates, too, favours Altabba's plan. Brandt's plan, he says, is completely uncharacteristic of Chinese building techniques and historically inaccurate.

Tang and Yang, however, point out one major disadvantage to both Brandt's and Altabba's plans: building the entire bridge on land requires space, and in a crowded urban waterfront or along a tight winding canal like this one there would be no room. The siting of the bridge had changed slightly from the original plan, exacerbating the space constraints and making the Americans' plans more difficult to implement. Their method solves the problem of space. Moreover, Tang and Yang feel the American proposals are too complex in the deployment; theirs, they say, offers simplicity and efficiency, and is more in line with ancient construction practices.

In the end, the home team wins the argument, and everyone agrees to use Tang's and Yang's plan to construct the rainbow bridge. The next day, however, a new argument erupts. Yang never mentioned that he planned to use steel bolts in addition to bamboo lashing to secure the joints. This again brings up the question of authenticity. Yang insists that safety concerns absolutely require the use of metal fasteners. Yates consults with Tang and points out that the Song had the most advanced iron and steel technology in the world. Historical records from the eleventh century indicate that iron nails were used in other bridges, so there is no reason why the Song couldn't have fashioned some type of iron nail to use in the construction of the rainbow bridge.

In the end, the NOVA team decides to use as authentic a nail as possible: a 12-inch iron clinch nail, which forks about 4 inches at the end, allowing it to be twisted around to secure the beam (rather like a brass paper fastener). In any case, most of the joints will be secured with bamboo lashing as planned. Peace is made, and there is a two-day break to wait for the nails to be forged and arrive on site.

During this break, Yates decides to investigate the bridge site, using the art of feng shui, or geomancy. As early as the Shang Dynasty, around 1500 BC, the Chinese had developed a system for aligning themselves, their buildings and other structures with respect to each other, to the cardinal directions and to the cosmos. The system was based on the belief that at every location artificial and natural topographical features indicate or modify the energy force, or *qi*, which flows through all things in the universe. The forms of hills, the directions of watercourses, the heights and shapes of buildings, the directions of roads and bridges, all are potent factors. To alter the natural direction of the *qi* can have serious consequences, positive or negative.

'By the time of the Song, feng shui had become a complex art,' says Robin Yates as he demonstrates a special compass called a *lo pan*. It's round, to symbolize heaven, with a square base to symbolize earth. Inside is a magnetic compass to

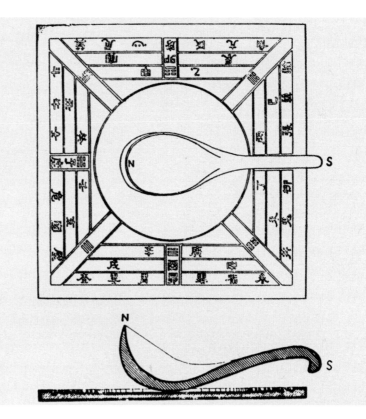

The lo pan, or feng shui compass, was the earliest form of the magnetic compass. Magnetic forces cause the spoon to rotate in the bowl.

ensure that buildings are properly aligned with the directions. Also on the compass are fourteen different rings, each with a different set of signs, such as the names of the twenty-eight lunar lodges – the Chinese equivalent of zodiac signs. By manipulating the compass it is possible to determine the appropriate location of a new structure or the most auspicious date to begin construction.

'I'm pleased about the location of our bridge,' Yates intones as he walks around the site with his compass. 'The Jinze canal flows north or south depending on the tide, and south is the most advantageous direction to face in feng shui. Also, there is a Buddhist temple and a large lake to the north of the site. Water is yin, or female, and you want that to your back. You want the yang, or male, in front of you. Unfortunately, to the southwest of the bridge is a toilet,' Yates observes. 'That toilet is yin and that's very inauspicious. We really should take down the toilet and put it up on the north side.'

Feng shui continues to be practised by millions of people today, and in recent years it has become popular with western urban professionals seeking to inject some *qi* into their personal lives. But by far its greatest impact on civilization has been through the invention of the magnetic compass, probably the most influential development of the Song Dynasty. Along with the sternpost rudder, the magnetic compass allowed the Song's great ocean-going ships to navigate with confidence far from shore. Adapted by Arab and later European sailors, these innovations transformed the course of world history.

It's a warm, sunny, humid day when the nails arrive and work begins on assembling the rainbow bridge. As if in celebration, Jinze is suddenly transformed. Hundreds of citizens parade through the narrow streets, led by a drummer and a cymbal player, flag holders, and lantern carriers. Singing and dancing troupes in bright red or pink outfits accompany the throng from temple to temple, as people stop inside each one to pray and burn offerings of yellow paper money. The scents of smoke and incense fill the air. Vendors are everywhere, taking advantage of the river of customers.

It is the advent of the 'Double Ninth' festival, held on the ninth day of the ninth month of the lunar calendar. The word for nine, *jiu*, is the same sound as the word for 'old' or 'long'. So on this holiday people pray in particular for longevity, for themselves and their families.

Down by the river long wooden poles are stacked on both banks. On each bank, workers take two long poles and tie them together near the top so they

Using shear legs and a block and tackle, the work crew hoists the H-shaped side section into place.

resemble an inverted V. Once upright, these 'shear legs' are tied back to stakes in the ground to make them stable.

'These shear legs give you a place to hang the block-and-tackle, or pulleys, so that your pulling force comes from up high,' Marcus Brandt explains. 'Block-and-tackle has been around for two or three thousand years.' He and his timber framer colleagues had used the same device in Scotland to lift the throwing arm of the NOVA team's trebuchets (see Chapter 1).

On the near bank, workers use the block-and-tackle to raise one of the preassembled H-shaped side sections. The bottom of the H section is wedged into the abutment, and the rest of it wobbles up into midair, positioned crookedly over the river. On the far side of the canal, crew members raise the other side section. Its precarious position makes the first one look straight. The two sections angle over the river from opposite sides. Below them, two flat-bottomed boats are moored out in the canal, holding the beams for the middle section that will complete the three-sided arch. The experts watching do not look confident.

'It looks very uneven,' Altabba points out. 'The right one is higher than the left. The only way to fit the middle piece is to get it exactly right. Tricky, but they may be able to do it.'

'It's a big challenge to assemble these pieces dangling in the air,' Brandt agrees. 'Until you get quite a few pieces put together, this thing is just a wobbly house of cards.'

The fact that one of the boats is sinking doesn't make the project easier. One worker is assigned the task of bailing water to keep it afloat.

The workers on the boats begin to lift one of the 200-pound beams that will connect the two side sections. Standing on sawhorse-shaped scaffolds, they use forked wooden poles to hold the beam in place between the two side sections. Other workers attach each end of the beam with the iron clinch nails. Then they hoist a second 200-pound beam and nail it into place, parallel to the first. All that remains is to position the crosspiece between the two parallel beams to form an H, and the centre section will be complete. The crosspiece is wrapped in bright red cloth for good luck, with firecrackers dangling from the sides. It's lifted up, the clinch nails go in, and the workers set off the firecrackers in celebration. Altabba shakes his head sceptically.

The three-sided arch is wobbly and uneven, but the addition of the four-sided arch woven into it should solidify it. At the moment, Brandt and Altabba reserve judgement. 'Well,' says Brandt, 'the geometry is pretty fixed now. Of course, using bamboo lashing alone, it would have been much, much more difficult.' Still, they agree that the nails are just an expedient; they will not hold the bridge up themselves once all the pieces are in place.

'What holds the bridge together are timbers pressing against each other,' Brandt explains. 'That's what makes this bridge strong. The fasteners just make erection easier. Once the bridge is up you could pull the fasteners out and the bridge would stand just fine.'

Brandt's comments reignite the debate over what sort of bridge this is.
According to Altabba, the action Brandt has just described is one of compressing forces. The definition of a beam, he says, is a member that is primarily bending and has little or no axial compression. An arch is the opposite: it is in compression and has little bending. 'If you apply that definition to the rainbow bridge,' he insists, 'there is no question. By definition it behaves like an arch.'

Workers hammer 12-inch iron clinch nails into the beams. The Song dynasty had the most advanced iron and steel technology in the world; long nails like these may have been used to secure the rainbow bridges of old.

Brandt still disagrees: 'I see it behaving uniquely to any of the models we've played with before. It's behaving not only as a beam, but as an arch. It's a bit of both.'

'It can't be both,' insists Altabba. 'It's either a beam or an arch. The confusion occurs from the fact that the pieces made of are straight pieces, and people associate straight pieces with beams regardless of how they behave. But if it looks like an arch, and it acts like an arch, I say it's an arch.'

The next morning the NOVA team assembles by the river to begin the delicate operation of weaving the four-sided arch into the three-sided one. It's raining lightly as construction workers bring two long beams to form the centre of the four-sided arch. Carefully, workers weave the long beams over and under the crosspieces as the joints of the three-sided arch. Two short beams supporting the two long ones form the base of the four-sided arch. Finally, workers lash the interwoven beams together at every juncture.

Pairs of timbers are woven over and under the cross-pieces of the three-sided arch. The construction is similar to that of a woven basket.

As the double-woven-arch structure begins to take shape, Tom Peters, the architect, is once again caught up in the classification debate. 'The thing looks more and more like a basket as it keeps on growing,' he remarks. 'And that is not a normal construction at all. It's a fascinating thing. Engineers do not have models to understand that kind of behaviour. Their models are for simple arches or beams or cantilevers or suspension systems, but they're not for interwoven systems that act in a multitude of different ways at once. These can be partly in bending or compression, or under different kinds of stresses than you get from a normal layered construction.

'The more I look at it, the more I think the inventor thought of this by looking at a basket turned on its side. He pressed down on it, and it didn't squash and it didn't move, and he thought, Well, why don't we do this to make a span? You can see how the forces spread through it in a different way than in a normal construction. It's a beautiful thing to watch.'

As aesthetically pleasing as the weaving process may be, when the top of the four-sided arch is completely woven in, there is a problem. Gaps as much as eight inches wide have appeared between the arches and the crosspieces, and the long beams do not meet in the middle to brace each other. The entire structure appears to be compromised. Tang speaks quietly but heatedly to the contractor.

'The geometry is way out,' Altabba shakes his head. 'That's one hell of a gap. This is a problem. It's going to be very difficult, probably impossible, to fit in the other pieces.'

'Normally you build things on top of each other,' Peters explains, 'and they hold together by gravity. This is the only instance I know when you're actually interweaving beams. It's more akin to the way cloth is made than to the way a building is made. As far as I know, this is unique in the history of construction. It forms a strong bond without the use of a whole lot of material. Very efficient once it's in place, but it's the devil to build, as you can see.'

The bridge looks like a matchstick model ready to collapse from the slightest agitation, but the Chinese workers seem completely unconcerned. They continue calmly to weave in the lower segments of the four-sided arch as the Double Ninth festival continues around them.

A worker uses a mallet to try to tap the beams into place. Gaps between the beams mean that the interwoven arches are not bracing one another properly.

With all the beams now in place, the westerners, despondent, head off for lunch at a local restaurant. When they return, they find that the building crew has apparently worked some sort of holiday magic. The eight-inch gaps between beams have nearly disappeared. An inch or less now separates the joints. When they find out the reason, the NOVA team members are flabbergasted. Without consulting the others, and with little regard for historical authenticity, the construction workers have simply forced the gaps together with steel bolts.

Altabba, the engineer, feels the bridge has been severely weakened. 'They basically forced the members together,' he says. 'And that's the worst thing you can do for this kind of structure. It induces all kinds of stresses in the members that weren't there. You want to build something geometrically correct, so it doesn't have any unnecessary stresses in it, so that all its force and capacity is reserved for when the load comes on. By forcing it in place, you've already consumed part of its capacity for stress.'

Drilling new holes through the wood to put in the steel bolts so close to the iron nails did even more damage, he argues. He wonders how heavy a load the bridge can now support.

'It probably won't fall down, probably not,' he says glumly. 'If anything the abutments will give way first.'

To timber framer Brandt, however, the Chinese workers' practices are perfectly viable. Wood is forgiving, he says: 'You can bend it, twist it, tweak it to get it to fit right – wood has so many forgiving qualities that I think what they did really isn't a problem. You know, engineers like reality to be close to their models. In a model, you're assuming joints are perfect, pieces are behaving in a known way. But the real world is different than that.'

Peters agrees: 'Think of the human body. It's never perfect. Everyone is a little asymmetrical, and yet the body functions. The bridge will adapt the same way.'

None of these disagreements seems to faze Tang, who has been waiting forty years for the chance to build a true rainbow bridge. 'The original rainbow bridge was built for the first time nine hundred years ago,' he beams. 'Now, we are building it again, like the one in the painting. This is a happy day for me.'

Amid these heated discussions, the double-arch framework is finally put in place. It soars across the canal indeed like a wooden rainbow. But the distinctive 'reverse curve' shape of the rainbow bridge is not yet visible. This will come from the installation of the decking – the surface that pedestrians will actually travel on.

The crew begins work on the decking on the day after the festival. It is a sunny, cool day, and Jinze has that morning-after look. Some small groups are still praying at the temples, but the streets are quiet, travelled by only a few early pedestrians and some windblown pieces of trash. The canal has turned an even darker brown-green from floating garbage.

In a few hours, the curved planks are secure, gently dipping, as seen in profile, in and out of the arched curve. Describing it, Tang echoes Tom Peters's metaphor of

The woven structure of the bridge is visible beneath the graceful curve of the decking.

the human form: 'This reverse curve is one of the most aesthetically pleasing of all curves. People of all nationalities feel this way, and I think it is because it is the human shape. The rainbow bridge curves just like a woman's body.'

The rainbow bridge is nearly complete. All that's left is to put up the railings, the stairs and the five reddish-brown ceramic dragon heads on each side. When this is done, the entire bridge is treated with oil from the tung tree to help preserve the wood and give it a rich, warm sheen. Finally, workers paint the railings red, as they've done since at least the Tang Dynasty. It's a good-luck colour used to ward off evil influences and makes the bridge stand out from a distance.

With the bridge finally standing, the NOVA team members look upon it with mixed feelings. Bashar Altabba sums it up best: 'This was a great experiment, and extremely interesting conceptually. Unfortunately, some questions have still not been resolved. Would the abutments as planned have worked? Would the geometry have worked without the steel bolts at the end?

'Still, look at it. The weaving pattern is beautiful, and the wood is so warm to look at. To recreate it from scratch, with no other ones in existence, is really something.'

Andrew Li needs no convincing. 'I have acquired an immense respect for the construction workers,' he says. 'It's amazing how sophisticated this thing was, how difficult it was to put together. There's a lesson for those of us who are office designers.'

Before people are allowed on the rainbow bridge, the NOVA team holds a ceremonial load test. With hundreds of villagers filling the banks of the canal to watch, farmers lead two massive *shuiniu*, or water buffalo, on to opposite ends of the bridge. The one-ton beasts with their foot-long horns daintily climb up the steps, pass each other at the top, and make their way down the other side.

'There wasn't the slightest sign of bending,' Altabba says happily. 'Not even the slightest squeak.'

Finally, performers take to the bridge to continue the festivities. Acrobats, drummers, a group of dancers in a colourful dragon costume, and musicians pack the bridge to capacity. A parade of boats pass underneath, carrying more musicians. The final boat carries Tang underneath the bridge, a moment of fulfilment of his forty-year dream.

While fireworks light up the sky, the members of the NOVA team are engulfed by villagers who have gathered to watch from the shore. Brandt and Altabba are relieved to note that the crowd of people packing the deck – their total weight far greater than those of the two water buffalo – aren't bending the rainbow arch an inch.

A troupe of acrobats crosses the newly completed bridge.

In 1234, a century after they routed the Northern Song, the Jin Dynasty was crushed by Mongol warriors under their ruthless leader, Ghengis Khan. The apotheosis of a thousand years of military prowess as mounted archers, the Mongol war machine had swept through most of Eurasia, devastating town after town, reducing great capitals to rubble. Now, after taking control of northern China, they set about conquering the Southern Song. The Song held out for over forty years, mainly through their superior naval forces, advanced gunpowder weaponry and strength of will, but eventually the Mongols were able to invade through the western interior and pillage their way to the sea. The last Song emperor died in a naval battle near present-day Hong Kong, and in 1279 Ghengis's ablest grandson, Kublai Khan, became emperor of all China, setting up the capital of the new Yuan ('Origin') Dynasty in Beijing.

China was the treasure house the Mongols ruthlessly exploited to fund the expansion of their empire. The Khans were after world domination, and they came pretty close, conquering India, Europe and Arabia in addition to China (although they failed to penetrate Japan). For the Chinese, the Mongol conquest marked the beginning of a 150-year dark age. The educated elite were lumped together with their fellow Chinese at the bottom of the social hierarchy, below the Mongols,

To test the load-bearing capacity of the bridge, a water buffalo is led across the bridge.

The entire village gathers on the bridge to celebrate its construction as boats carrying celebrants pass below.

their allies and other foreign groups. Under foreign rule, China's meritocratic examination system disappeared for over a century, as did many of the Song's intellectual practices and economic reforms. Among the treasures lost for ever was the technique of building rainbow bridges.

The disappearance of the rainbow bridge, notes Robin Yates, is as mysterious as its origins. Though the Ruzhen or the Mongols may have destroyed the bridge in Kaifeng, such destruction, he says, rarely brought with it the extinction of an art.

'The Mongols were keen on Chinese craftsmen,' Yates explains. 'They would massacre an entire town's population, but keep the artisans alive and take them with them. That's probably how gunpowder and the cannon were transferred to the West, for example.' But for some reason, the original design of this bridge was lost.

Yates notes that the bridge required large timbers; with the deforestation of China's plains, the material with which to build such bridges disappeared. That may be why the bridge's descendants are found today only in mountainous, well-forested regions.

'My suspicion,' offers Altabba, 'is that the level of complexity involved in the erection of the rainbow bridge made it not as popular, even though it was elegant and efficient.' Whatever the reason, the secrets of the bridge were lost in the thundering hoofbeats of the Mongol chargers.

Today, many of our modern bridges are based on principles established by Chinese craftsmen a millennium or more ago. But though the principles endure, human civilization will never recreate that moment in the great Song Dynasty, when a man looked across the Bien Canal and imagined a new way of crossing it, with bold swoops and wood woven like cloth and a reverse curve arching over the water like a timbered wave.

References

books

Chevedden, P. E., L. Eigenbrod, V. Foley and W. Soedel, 'The Trebuchet', *Scientific American*, July 1995

Corfis, I. A., and M. Wolfe, *The Medieval City under Siege.* Boydell Press, Woodbridge (UK), 1995

Gies, J. and F. Gies, *Life in a Medieval Castle.* Harper and Row, New York, 1974

Needham, J., R. D. S. Yates, K. Gawlikowski, E. McEwen and W. Ling, *Science and Civilization in China*; Vol. 5, Part VI: *Military Technology, Missiles and Sieges.* Cambridge University Press, Cambridge, 1994

Prestwich, M., *Armies and Warfare in the Middle Ages.* Yale University Press, New Haven, 1996

websites

TIMBER FRAMERS' GUILD
http://www.tfguild.org/worktreb.html
A report on the Timber Framers' four-day effort to build and test-fire a fixed-weight trebuchet at the Virginia Military Institute.

http://www.tfguild.org/fling.html
This site gives a day-by-day account of the NOVA trebuchet experiment.

ARMEDIEVAL
http://members.xoom.com/montjoie/armed_en.html
This site is a guide to exhibits and demonstrations and shows images and descriptions of medieval weapons reconstructed by ARMEDIEVAL under the direction of Renaud Beffeyte. Armedieval is an enterprise of carpentry originally devoted to traditional constructions and restorations, and has specialized since 1984 in reconstituting the machines produced by civil and military engineers of the Middle Ages and the Renaissance.

GREY COMPANY
http://www.iinet.net.au/~rmine/histreb.html
http://www.iinet.net.au/~rmine/histrac.html
This provides historical images of different types of trebuchets and information about how they worked, along with links to other trebuchet-related websites. The Grey Company is a pageantry group that focuses on the so-called Dark Ages (600-1100 AD)

BOOKS

Budge, E. A. Wallis, *Cleopatra's Needles and Other Egyptian Obelisks.*
Dover Publications, New York, 1990

Clarke, Somers, and R. Engelbach, *Ancient Egyptian Construction and Architecture.*
Dover Publications, New York, 1990

Dibner, Bern, *Moving the Obelisks.* MIT Press, Cambridge, 1970

Engelbach, Reginald, *The Aswan Obelisk, With Some Remarks on the Ancient
Engineering.* Imprimerie de L'Institut Français, Cairo, 1922

Engelbach, Reginald, *The Problem of the Obelisks.* George H. Doran,
New York, 1923

Habachi, Labib, *The Obelisks of Egypt: Skyscrapers of the Past.* The American
University in Cairo Press, Cairo, 1984

Partridge, Robert, *Transport in Ancient Egypt.* Rubicon Press, London, 1996

Vinson, Steve, *Egyptian Boats and Ships.* Shire Publications,
Buckinghamshire, 1994

websites

NOVA ONLINE ADVENTURE: MYSTERIES OF THE NILE
http://www.pbs.org/wgbh/nova/egypt
The official website of the Obelisk II project, including dispatches from the field
and biographies of the investigators.

THE THEBAN MAPPING PROJECT
http://www.kv5.com
The official website of KV5, an exciting new excavation led by archaeologist Kent
Weeks, takes you inside this tomb with movies, QuickTime VRs and maps. The
site also offers a tour of Thebes, an overview of the Valley of the Kings and an
excellent introduction to Egyptology.

THE AMERICAN RESEARCH CENTER IN EGYPT – ARCE
http://www.arce.org/home.html
The ARCE is the professional society in the United States of specialists on Egypt
of all periods. The site provides information on the latest programmes, events,
projects, local ARCE chapters, research opportunities, resources and publications.

THE ORIENTAL INSTITUTE
http://www-oi.uchicago.edu/OI/default.html
The Oriental Institute is a museum and research organization devoted to the study
of the archaeology, philology and history of early Near Eastern civilizations.

THE AMERICAN SCHOOLS OF ORIENTAL RESEARCH – ASOR
http://www.asor.org/
ASOR's mission is to initiate, encourage and support research and public
understanding of the peoples and cultures of the Near East from the earliest times.
On their page, you can find out more about their education programme, events,
overseas centres, publications, excavations and other resources.

EGYPTOLOGY RESOURCES
http://www.newton.cam.ac.uk/egypt/index.html
The Newton Institute in the University of Cambridge maintains this website of
Egyptology resources. The site includes news, bulletins, organizations and other
related resources.

IN ITALY ONLINE – CHASING OBELISKS IN ROME
http://www.initaly.com/regions/classic/obelisks.htm
This page offers a short history of thirteen obelisks in Rome.

KARNAK
http://interoz.com/egypt/karnak.htm
The Egyptian Ministry of Tourism has put together an informative site that offers
a comprehensive history of Karnak.

BOOKS

Davis, Tom, and Pa Tuterangi Ariki, *Vaka: Saga of a Polynesian Canoe.* Institute of Pacific Studies/Polynesian Press, University of the South Pacific/Samoa House, Rarotonga and Suva/Auckland, 1992

Dos Passos, John, *Easter Island – Island of Enigmas.* Doubleday & Company, New York, 1971

Heyerdahl, Thor, *Kon-Tiki: Across the Pacific By Raft.* Pocket Books, New York,1950

Heyerdahl, Thor, *Easter Island: The Mystery Solved.* Random House, New York, 1989

Kane, Herb Kawainui, *Voyagers.* WhaleSong Inc., Bellevue, Washington, 1991

Lewis, David, *We, the Navigators: The Ancient Art of Landfinding in the Pacific.* University of Hawaii Press, Honolulu, 1994

Orliac, Catherine and Michel, *Easter Island: Mystery of the Stone Giants.* Harry N. Abrams Inc., New York, 1995

Routledge, Mrs Scoresby (Katharine Routledge), *The Mystery of Easter Island – The Story of an Expedition.* Sifton, Praed & Co., London, 1919

Sharp, Andrew, *The Journal of Jacob Roggeveen.* Oxford University Press, Oxford, 1970

Van Tilburg, Jo Anne and John Mack, *Easter Island: Archaeology, Ecology, and Culture.* Smithsonian Institution Press, Washington, DC, 1995

websites

EASTER ISLAND

http://www.mysteriousplaces.com/Easter_Island/index.html

Take a virtual tour of Easter Island. This site features beautiful photography
of *moai*.

KON-TIKI WEB SERVER

http://www.media.uio.no/Kon-Tiki/

Explore scholarly papers from Norway's Kon-Tiki Museum and enjoy a welcome
from Thor Heyerdahl himself.

POLYNESIAN VOYAGING SOCIETY

http://leahi.kcc.hawaii.edu/org/pvs

Find out about this organization, which investigates how the Polynesian seafarers
discovered and settled the islands of the Pacific. Learn what it's like to live for a
month on board a replica of an ancient voyaging canoe.

RAPANUI

http://www2.hawaii.edu/~ogden/piir/pacific/Rapanui.html

A paper on the people, government, economy, history and more of Easter Island.
This site includes many useful resources for visitors.

RAPA NUI OUTRIGGER CLUB

http://www.netaxs.com/~trance/outrig.html

An organization, founded by Jo Anne Van Tilburg, that gives young Rapa Nui
people the opportunity to learn about their people's history while developing
outrigger canoe paddling skills.

OFFICIAL EASTER ISLAND HOME PAGE

http://www.netaxs.com/~trance/rapanui.html

Information on Easter Island's history, culture and tourism. Check out the great
list of web links.

ZVI SHILLER'S HOMEPAGE

http://www.seas.ucla.edu/~shiller

Read about Zvi Shiller's motion planning research and how it was applied to the
NOVA *moai*-moving experiment.

BOOKS

Adam, J.-P., *Roman Building*. Indiana University Press, Bloomington, Indiana, 1994

Aicher, P. J., *Guide to the Aqueducts of Ancient Rome*. Bolchazy-Carducci, Wauconda, Illinois, 1995

Colman, P., *Toilets, Bathtubs, Sinks and Sewers*. Atheneum, New York, 1994

De Bonneville, F., *The Book of the Bath*. Rizzoli, New York, 1998

De Camp, L. S., *The Ancient Engineers*. Doubleday, New York, 1963

DeLaine, J., *The Baths of Caracalla*, Roman Archaeology supplementary series, Portsmouth, RI 1997

Fagan, G. G., *Bathing in Public in the Ancient World*. University of Michigan Press, Michigan, 1999

Toner, J. P., *Leisure and Ancient Rome*. Polity Press, Cambridge, UK, 1995

Yegül, F. K., *The Bath-Gymnasium Complex at Sardis*. Harvard University Press, Cambridge, Massachusetts, 1986

Yegül, F. K., *Baths and Bathing in Classical Antiquity*. Harvard University Press, Cambridge, Massachusetts, 1992

websites

ANCIENT BATHS RESOURCE SITE
http://www3.la.psu.edu/cams/baths/baths.html
This site, maintained by Garrett Fagan, offers a gallery of images, information, and resources on Roman baths.

THE ROMAN BATHS MUSEUM AND PUMP ROOM (Bath, England)
http://www.romanbaths.co.uk
A virtual tour and slide show of the Roman baths and temple at Bath, England.

PUBLIC BATHS OF POMPEII
http://www.bowdoin.edu/dept/clas/arch304/baths/index.html
Views and descriptions of the Roman baths at Pompeii.

BOOKS

Cotterell, Brian and Johan Kamminga, *Mechanics of Pre-Industrial Technology.* Cambridge University Press, Cambridge. 1991

Coyne, Peter, 'China's Historic Bridges: An enduring link with the past'. *Arts of Asia,* May/June 1989

Coyne, Peter, 'Carpenters of the Rainbow', *Archaeology,* March/April 1992

Elvin, Mark, *Pattern of the Chinese Past.* Stanford University Press, Stanford, California, 1973

Fairbank, John King, *China: A New History.* Harvard University Press, Cambridge, Massachusetts, 1992

Gies, Joseph, *Bridges and Men.* Doubleday, New York, 1963

Heren, Louis, C. P. Fitzgerald, Michael Freeberne, Brian Hook and David Bonavia, *China's Three Thousand Years.* Collier Books, New York, 1973

Institute of the History of Natural Sciences, Chinese Academy of Sciences, *Ancient China's Technology and Science.* Foreign Language Press, Beijing, 1983

Knapp, Ronald, *Chinese Bridges.* Oxford University Press, Hong Kong, 1993

Needham, Joseph, *Science and Civilization in China.* Cambridge University Press, various dates and editions

websites

ANCIENT BRIDGES
http://bridge.tongji.edu.cn/bridges/ancient/ancient.htm
A great overview of the ancient bridges of China. From Tonji University, home of
Professor Yang of the Rainbow Bridge Project.

HISTORY OF CHINA
http://fractal.umd.edu/history/toc.html
A good history of China, with exhaustive bibliography to lead you to
further study.

THE SCIENCE AND CIVILIZATION IN CHINA PROJECT
http://www.soas.ac.uk/needham/SCC
A comprehensive overview and update of the massive book project started by the
late historian Joseph Needham.

Numbers in *italic* refer to illustrations

Courtesy of WGBH/NOVA: 146, 195

    Michael Barnes: 20, 32, 36, 37, 39, 40 (right), 44, 49, 51, 95, 126, 177, 193

    Liesl Clark: 4-5, 16-17, 98, 100-01, 102, 105, 106, 110, 111, 128, 132

    Deborah J. Fryer: 14, 135, 137, 143, 149, 152, 153, 154-55,
        156, 157, 158, 159, 160, 161, 162, 164, 165, 167, 169, 171

    Brendan Kootsey: 99, 129, 130, 131

    Mark Lehner: 61, 63, 78, 79, 80

    Jackie Mow: 13, 172, 173, 174 (bottom), 178, 179, 181, 182, 183, 196, 199, 200,
        201, 202, 203, 205, 206, 207, 208-09

    Neoscape: 150, 166

    Michael Prendergast: 82, 84, 85, 90, 118, 119, 128

    Peter Tyson: 2, 8, 17, 54, 55, 58, 60, 62, 65, 72, 73, 76, 96, 97

    Wang Zu Ji: 174-5

Album de Villard De Honnecourt Architecture du XIII Siècle Manuscrit Publiè en Fac-Simile, Leonce
    Laget, Paris 1976: 35

British Library, Neg. No. 41496, Shelfmark Cott.Nero.D.11, folio 191v: 22

© The British Museum: 109, 138

Courtesy of the Freer Gallery of Art, Smithsonian Institution,
    Washington, D.C. Acc.#F1954.21-6: 188

Giraudon/Art Resource, NY: 184

Attributed to Emperor Huizong, Chinese (1082-1135). Handscroll; ink, colour and gold on silk;
    H x W: 14 5/8 x 57 3/16 in (37 x 145.3 cm) Special Chinese and Japanese Fund, 12.886.
    Courtesy, Museum of Fine Arts, Boston: 186

Hulton Getty/Liaison Agency: 108

Courtesy of Vince Lee: 116, 122, 124

Courtesy of Mark Lehner: 57, 68, 87, 88, 89, 92, 95

© Walter Leonardi/Sebra Film: 107

Courtesy of Ed Levin: 33, 34

Erich Lessing/Art Resource, NY: 140

Courtesy of Terri Manooghan: 21, 24, 42, 43, 45, 46-47

Mary Evans Picture Library: 103

Needham, *Science and Civilisation in China*, vol. 4, part 1, Cambridge University
    Press 1962: 185, 198

P.E. Newberry, *El Bersheh*. London: Egypt Exploration Society, Archaeological Survey of Egypt,
    1892: 66

Courtesy of Niedersächsische Staats und Universitäts Bibliothek Göttingen: 29

© Patrimonio Nacional. Madrid: 10, 34 (top)

Edmond Paulin, Thermes de Dioclétien, Envoi de 1880 Ecole Nationale Superièure des
    Beaux-Arts, Paris: 142

Payne-Gallwey, Sir Ralph, *The Projectile-Throwing Engines of the Ancients*, Rowman and Littlefield,
    Totowa, New Jersey, 1973: 41

Courtesy of Keith Rodgerson: 170

Routledge, Katherine Scoresby, *The Mystery of Easter Island: The Story of an Expedition*, London: 112

Scala/Art Resource, NY: 25

Siege of Antioch (1097-98) by William of Tyre (c. 1130-1185), Estoire d'Outremer
    (12th Century), Bibliotheque Municipale de Lyon/Bridgeman Art Library: 28

© Lee Snider/Photo Images: 134

© Roger Viollet/Liaison Agency: 71

© Patrick Ward/Chameleon Photos: 50

Werner Forman/Art Resource, NY: 147

Courtesy of Wil Wilkins: 40 (left), 48

Acknowledgements

This book is the product of the labour of many people. First and foremost, we are grateful to Caroline Chauncey at WGBH for her immeasurable help and advice. We are also indebted to Kay Hale and Helen Albertson of the RSMAS Library at the University of Miami and to the staff of the Orleans Public Library on Cape Cod. Amy Carzo and Susan Lee Butts of WGBH also deserve credit for cheerfully tying up loose ends.

We gratefully acknowledge clarifications from Michael Prestwich (*Medieval Siege*); Mark Lehner (*Pharaoh's Obelisk*); Georgia Lee (*Easter Island*); Garrett Fagan and Peter Aicher (*Roman Bath*); and Robin Yates (*China Bridge*). We also appreciate clarifications from and interviews with Renaud Beffeyte (*Medieval Siege*); Vince Lee (*Easter Island*); Tony Rook, Max Fordham, and Fikret Yegül (*Roman Bath);* and Bashar Altabba (*China Bridge*).

This book could never have happened without the assistance of the talented and award-winning producers of Mysteries of Lost Empires: Michael Barnes, executive producer (*Medieval Siege* and *China Bridge*); Liesl Clark (*Easter Island*); Julia Cort (*Pharaoh's Obelisk*); and Nancy Linde (*Roman Bath*), along with their assistant producers Marti Louw, Jackie Mow, Kate Churchill, Mary Brockmyre, and Diana Dresser, and production assistant Julie Crawford, whose daily dispatches from China were indispensable. Peter Tyson of NOVA also provided invaluable material. Paula S. Apsell is the executive producer of the NOVA Science Unit, whose support made *Mysteries of Lost Empires* possible.

The TV series *Mysteries of Lost Empires* is a NOVA Production by the WGBH Science Unit in association with Channel 4 in Britain and La Cinquième in France. NOVA is produced for PBS by the WGBH Science Unit. Major funding for NOVA is provided by the Park Foundation, The Northwestern Mutual Life Foundation, and CNET, along with the Corporation for Public Broadcasting and public television viewers. Additional funding for *Mysteries of Lost Empires* was provided by the David H. Koch Charitable Foundation.